Happy Mother's Day '84

With much love from

Phil xx Charles xx

Sunday Best

by the same author

KITCHEN IN THE CORNER
ROUNDABOUT
ONLY ON SUNDAYS
WHITEHORN'S SOCIAL SURVIVAL
OBSERVATIONS
HOW TO SURVIVE IN HOSPITAL
HOW TO SURVIVE CHILDREN

Sunday Best

KATHARINE WHITEHORN

EYRE METHUEN LTD

11 NEW FETTER LANE LONDON EC4P 4EE

First published in 1976 by Eyre Methuen Ltd
11 New Fetter Lane, London EC4P 4EE

Printed in Great Britain
by Butler & Tanner Ltd, Frome and London

ISBN 0 413 36810 6

For my Father,
as A. E. Housman said of Trinity,
'ancient, liberal, humane and
my most kindly nurse'.

Acknowledgements

My thanks are due to the editor of *The Observer*, in which these articles first appeared.

K. W.

Contents

Introduction

I have a friend who is a brain surgeon, who takes me out to lunch now and then; when he does, he is always full of wonder at the way I earn my living.

'You writer people!' he marvels. 'Every week! Don't know how you do it. When I have to write something for *The Lancet*, it's torture. Up every night for weeks till two in the morning . . .'

'But John,' I say, 'that's my trade. I'm not too good at cutting into people's skulls, if it comes to that.'

'Oh, that.' He brushes it aside. 'That's easy. A monkey could do it, with the right training. But writing!'

Which just goes to show how impenetrable one person's trade is to another; and not all the mistakes are that flattering. Some people, for example, assume that columnists sit down for a couple of days and polish off enough columns to last six months. Would that we could; but there are good reasons why we don't. For one thing, time marches on: the people we write about may have been shot or found in bed with an Archbishop or otherwise discontinued – or the people we're writing *for* may have been. For another, the urge that makes editors think news is exciting also ensures that anything that's been kicking around the office for more than three weeks feels as dead to them as if it actually had been set, printed and wrapped around the geranium cuttings. But the main reason is that the difference between journalists and real writers is that we *can't* work until it's very nearly too late already. If we could, we would no doubt attempt to write the Bible or the *Decline and Fall of the British Empire* or one of those three-generation, three-volume three-joke novels, and you can be grateful we don't.

The opposite myth, of course, is that Sunday columnists put the last full stop after the last sentence at about teatime on Saturday. A few commentators on sports or politics (if you can distinguish the two) may do so, and reporters turn in copy late in the day; but the mechanics of newspapers are such that much of the typesetting has to be done a good deal earlier in the week, to leave the chaps free on Saturdays for the really urgent stuff. Over the years that these pieces came out in *The Observer*, the deadline's varied – never earlier than Tuesday lunchtime, rarely later than Thursday afternoon; it depended partly on the printing situation, partly on whether I was racing the copy to a last-minute lunatic who liked living dangerously or an organisation woman who would prefer to know what was happening on Tuesday in a year's time. They aren't often written in the office, which is far too full of intrigue, friends, the tea trolley, things to try on from the fashion department and people asking why you haven't accounted for your expenses since last July. I yield to no one in my admiration for the office as a social centre, but it's no place actually to get any work done.

Also it lacks one essential amenity: my husband. Gavin Lyall was a journalist before he started going straight as a thriller-writer and he edits my stuff before it gets out of the house. Occasionally he says 'That's fine' – meaning either that it really is OK or that it's so frightful he can't recommend anything that can be done with it. Anything polite, that is. More often he points out that this fact is wrong, or that sentence has been going on for a page and a half; or that I have inadvertently left out the main point of the article; on a really black day he asks what *is* the main point of the article. Only once, I think, has his influence been unfortunate, when he made me water down some unkind remarks about Mary Whitehouse (lest I be written off as a mindless hysteric) to such a point that several people thought I approved of her. Generally he improves things (he made me rewrite the one on going to Greece with my father five times); if *The Observer* ever realised how much he works for them I suppose they'd either have to pay him or shoot him.

The other question people ask is, 'How do you find something to write about each week?' or, more nastily, 'Isn't it sometimes *very difficult* to find something . . .?' Some ideas, of course, come out of things like conferences or interviews or books or lawsuits; more come from talking to people – that, and being for some reason held down in a situation of such invincible boredom that there is no alternative but to think. Fortunately my generation is well protected against this ghastly possibility, since we had to learn so much poetry by heart at school, and we can always recite it in our heads during traffic jams and annual reports, summaries from The Chair and those interminable international speeches that are dictated in Russia, spouted in Hungarian and delivered by crackling simultaneous translation: how people ever get through these without internal recitation is beyond me.

Be that as it may, if you should be stuck in a lift between two floors, I hope this fate will not have to overtake you. I hope you will have this book with you. By slapping it loudly against the walls of the lift, you may attract someone's attention; and then I shall feel that it has all been worth while.

Sorting Out

I have just discovered I have biodegradable handwriting – biodegradable being the OK pollution word for things which obligingly rot away by themselves, unlike the perpetual plastic cartons wrapped around Mr Heath's outboard motor. After I can no longer remember what was the subject of my scribble – say about two years – I can't read it, either. (The fact that other people can't read it at all is actually an advantage: I can gaze into a man's eyes while writing 'Shifty expression, hair in nose' with impunity.) But after a week of clearing out sack after sack of what is laughingly known as my filing system, I think we need a speed-up in the rate at which paper itself collapses.

I suppose we all share this pipe-dream of being able to reach out a hand and find anything at will; what is amazing is that we think that good filing could somehow make it come true. On the contrary: putting a letter into a filing system is like releasing your ferret in the Hampton Court maze.

Filing is concerned with the past; anything you actually need to see again has to do with the future. The more a thing is filed away, the more totally useless it is. A sweet disorder in the desk at least ensures that the whole thing is ploughed through often enough for useful things to come to the surface, while a letter in the files will stay there until disturbed by your executors. Unless, of course, you can cope with what Stevie Smith called 'the job-job-job of tearing up old letters. But that involves [the boss] who gets bored quickly like me by fool unnecessary jobs that are not at all asking to be done.'

You might think that the super-secretaries have systems that you or I might adopt. But when I started ringing round among them, I found that, to a woman, they laughed uneasily and said well, actually, filing wasn't exactly their strong point. One CBI secretary simply turfs everything into a large basket under her desk; a Unilever director's handmaiden said disarmingly 'Well, I keep the things we need oftenest nearest the front.' Several said they'd been taught elaborate systems at college which they'd never used, because every office has its own; and another said that though the theory is that a good system can be worked by anybody, in practice it can't, because you have to know whether in the mind of your predecessor a thing would come under the company, the man's name, the product or the problem.

The thing that is wrong with this streamlined filing we all aspire to is that it ignores the real nature of memory. Take chronology: it's far easier to remember that a thing happened last summer or three years ago than what the blasted man's name was. If you do 'file' in large piles of untreated sludge, you can find things the way geologists do; establishing the date by things like 1969 bulb catalogues and buried boiled sweets in different stages of *rigor mortis*. Sherlock Holmes, in 'The Private Life of,' ticks his housekeeper off for dusting: 'the dust is an integral part of my filing system.' 'But it was *that thick*!' she showed him. 'Hmm,' said the master, 'that would be 1876.' Precisely.

Again, most people's memory is visual. We rush out and buy identical grey folders that tell the memory nothing, when what we really need is containers of all shapes and sizes. Mrs Haro files in a soup tureen – now that's what I call memorable: one man said he drew an elephant on his Lest We Forget file; my Social Effects of TV one is simply an old handout folder made of jolly peasant *toile de jouy* wallpaper, with a TV aerial added to the odd castle or cottage. A girl who once worked for *Nova* used to have to keep files on the writers; she found their faces more memorable than their names, and would file a big-nosed contributor under N for Nose.

Another thing that makes our normal attempts at system so hopeless is that we try to be too precise. If you have six files with labels like 'Bills – home', 'Receipts 1969–70', 'Bank Statements' and so on, you'll never put anything in them; one big open-mouth called MONEY might well swallow them all. Sometimes you want to keep a newspaper clipping; if you really think you're going to paste it into a book, you're kidding yourself; bulldog paper-clips are the only answer. Brigid Keenan has a lovely concertina file that she uses for everything, clearing it out every two months – except, of course, that it fills up in three days and the rest is in carrier-bags like anyone else's.

Women, particularly, make trouble for themselves by not owning up to the things that are never going to come in handy; they are just there as mementoes (when I am 80 I propose to go to bed for the rest of my life with all the suitcases called Archives). And this stuff, you don't want to sort: you want deliberately to leave it unsorted, so that you see all the bits every time you have to hunt for something. Archives apart, most women need six files. These include one for medical cards and health records. One womb-to-tomb file for your birth certificate, will, insurance policies, passport. One called Future, to stop you frantically hunting for the address you're going to, while your husband revs the car *con brio*; and the vital one for instructions and guarantees on appliances. We used to keep all this in one top drawer in the days when we had a plan chest, and then we *always* knew where to find them.

But you never know, of course, what personal functions other people's systems may have. I told Bernard Levin I was giving up keeping theatre programmes in shoe boxes. 'Oh, I couldn't do that,' he said, shocked. 'When it's full, that's the only way I know I need a new pair of shoes.'

The Games Parents Play

This list of family games is by no means exhaustive but enough is enough. . . .

Creative hide-and-seek. Parent arranges paint, clay, sand, water, paste, paper, etc., while child evades capture and tries to make for 'home' – i.e., chair in front of TV.

My Word. Grown-up equivalent of the game children play, where questions must be answered without saying Yes, No, Black or White. In this case 'me' must be avoided; 'children' used instead, e.g., 'He plays golf all weekend and doesn't see enough of – the children'; 'I'm having a terrible time at work, she ought to be at home more, looking after – the children.'

Park Cricket played one-ended; umpire gives four if someone throws your ball back, six if you get it into a pram, out if it gets stuck in tree. Players can be given out not only Leg Before Wicket, but Thigh Before Tree, and Starting Before Ready; play is terminated by Business Before Pleasure.

Progressive Patience. In this game the parent goes on gently reasoning with an under-five as it kicks the furniture, scratches its brother and empties ashtrays over the carpet; loser is the first one who says BECAUSE I BLOODY WELL SAY SO and heaves child from room. Most popular as a spectator sport.

Touchline Football played by mothers at the edge of the field. Their sons pursue the ball as if wading through deep treacle, occasionally falling over if anything exciting begins to happen. Mothers cry 'After it, Jeremy!' or 'Go on, Crispin!' while compulsively jerking their own ankles. Referee intervenes if mothers actually invade the pitch.

Last-across, a game played by Mummies racing across zebra crossing with children, while Daddies, in big cars, try to run them down.

Steeplechasing or the loneliness of the long-distance mother, who assuages guilt about sending children to boarding school by choosing places at immense distances from one another. What with speech days, half terms, open days and the motorway, she manages to be almost as exhausted in term time as in the holidays.

Loo Snooker. Unsuccessful attempts to pot the white, or, in the case of Africans, the black.

Sing a Song of Sixpence. Parent describes pocket money, bedtimes, fewness of toys, length of time between treats and general austerity of own upbringing; use of phrase 'when I was your age' disqualifies.

Granddaughter's Footsteps. Adult sneaks out of playgroup, freezing instantly if child looks round; if child sees her move, she has to come back into the room and start again.

Draughts. Like the above, except that child attempts to leave room undetected; if he's seen, parent shouts DOOR! and child must return to room.

Miss the Pantomime. Mothers sidle up and down aisles as one after another child needs the lavatory; most apt to win (i.e., miss the whole show) are those who take fourteen children and forget to drain any of them beforehand.

Any Questions? Abstracted mother says 'yes' and 'no' alternately to all questions until one contains query about sex. She then removes apron, sits down and treats child to ten minutes' careful talk on how sex is just an ordinary part of life. Game ensures that children are quite certain it can't be, if this is the effect it has on Mother.

Speak, Piggy, Speak. Word game for teaching speech. Daddy says 'Bottle!' holds up bottle; child says nothing. Daddy picks up glass, says 'Glass!'; child still silent. Daddy drops glass, says 'Bugger!'; child instantly says 'Bugger, bugger, bugger'.

Call my Bluff. Parents define the world, giving about two false for one true definition; children must guess which is which. Bluff generally called once and for all at about age fourteen.

What I Said Was . . . I

Your fiancée? *Well – yes, sure . . . only she's . . . I mean she's been a very popular girl, that's all; I don't know if she'll settle down to country life very easily . . .*

So I said, she's had more men through her than the Mersey Tunnel, old boy, but if you want her, I said . . .

Friends . . . Hhrmph . . . friends . . . FRIENDS . . . ah that's better. . . . First of all I did – ah – want to thank you for coming here; on occasions like this I always say . . . of course, there's never been an occasion quite like this but any burial is a solemn thing . . . and I want to say here and now that I'm not a believer in de mortuis nil nisi bonum: *I'm not one to praise a man just because he's . . . I mean, it is no intention of mine to open old wounds . . .*

Friends, Romans, Countrymen! Lend me your ears
I come to bury Caesar, not to praise him. . . .

Faster, Faster

It has long been my boast that I can read or eat anything. But unfortunately, although I eat like a Hoover, I read so slowly that I am always on the smart book three years after everyone else has finished. It was bad enough when it was the Alan Mooreheads; but this year, despair at ever finishing John Updike's *Couples*, which I have been reading ever since I can remember, has finally driven me to a quicker-reading course.

I had better say at once that I was not their star pupil. They did bump up my speed (though I never got back my 100 per cent comprehension) and they never claim to do more than improve you at your own level. But I have not Changed My Attitude. I envy as much as ever the ones who read fast by nature; but at the end of the course I feel not so much how marvellous it is to read quickly, but how idiotic we are to put up with having so much to read.

This was a business reading course and they didn't claim it would enable you to race through *Crime and Punishment* in an hour and a half; the idea is more to flick the facts off a handout page like an ant-eater's tongue. It is designed for the mass of gump that arrives on the executive desk and somehow has to be got off it again; and for 75 per cent of that, they say, 75 per cent comprehension is enough.

But if it *is* enough to three-quarters-understand it, can it have been all that necessary to read it at all? You can't choose a factory site or assess a sales area on a three-quarters right appraisal of its merits. Sure, you will re-check something that you know is important – but what about the misconceptions you don't even know you have absorbed?

I get a mound of stuff on my desk, too, and when I'm looking for a subject I often stare at the Institutional Management Magazine, *Sweden Now*, or the effusions of the Footwear Council like someone looking at a beetroot and two tins of chestnuts desperately trying to think up a meal. But if I should use some of it in an article, would 75 per cent comprehension be enough? The mind boggles at the number of experts who would write in to denounce me.

Again, the technique is much recommended for reading newspapers. Well, I write for newspapers, dammit, and I don't agree. On the contrary: what horrifies me is the way people misunderstand what the papers say – any journalist knows that a controversial article will produce letters not only from those who think you have said the exact opposite of what you did say, but those who kindly continue your argument, repeating exactly the points you were making in the first place. Where quick reading keeps up your understanding, it's fine; but the understanding is surely far more important than the speed.

And if you bolt your food, you may not taste that it's poisoned. What the whole thing leaves out, it seems to me, is the question of *style*, and I am quite sure that, even in newspapers, style is also part of what is said. The course discourages vocalisation, for example. Suppose you didn't say over in your head a quotation like, 'My husband, 52, a steel welder, said to me . . .' would you instinctively realise that the rest of the quotation was probably bogus, too?

The disgruntled reader can well complain that there's no time to read anything properly – but writing properly is at least a possible answer. We are entirely too permissive, it seems to me, on the matter of length. The course listed three speeds – a fast one for fiction or your own subject; something slightly slower for unfamiliar reading, and a slower one still for White Papers – and someone unkindly added a tortoise rate for Capital Gains Tax.

What's so different about White Papers? That no one ever tries to keep them down to size. The Challoner Report ran to one million words; I simply don't believe it can have taken that many to say it. If you have to find out about a new subject in a hurry, it's fatal to start reading anything, because if you ask the great man to give you the gist of his 500-page work in a few sentences he almost always can. Indeed, it's a sign of greatness to be able to say, like D. W. Brogan, 'There is not a principle of politics which I cannot explain to a docker in half an hour.'

And take the novel. Here's *Couples*, 500 pages if it's a word, and no good skipping, because even if it's mouth to right breast on page 280 and mouth to left breast on 284, it may well be a different Couple by then or even (just to confuse you) half the first Couple Coupling with someone else. Do we really have to know about all of it? *Some* selectivity must come into it, after all, or the book would be eight million pages long – so why not a bit more, and help people like me along?

One of the great benefactors of mankind, a Scribner's editor, cut a third off *From Here to Eternity* – but it would still take me from here to eternity to finish it: why did he stop there? Habit, that's all; people write what they think is 'book length' and I'm delighted to hear that printing costs may be bringing book size down again.

It's just too bad that newspapers have to be big for economic reasons. I offered to leave my column space blank this week to help the slow readers, but they simply thought I was slacking. Still, I'd like you to know the thought was there.

Decoding the West

There are times when I think I have seen more Westerns than any other woman alive. Maybe it only seems like this because it's all been crammed into the mere dozen years since I said: 'Thy country shall be my country and thy people my people' and we both clearly understood that what we meant was the West; but it's been a long, long trail.

In the early days we would travel fifty minutes in the Tube to catch *Winchester 73*, she for the first time, he for the tenth, as they say in *Time*; or ride a series of buses into Essex in the rain to hear that ghastly freckled child say 'Shay-ane!' yet once more. But television improved things, and the unceasing efforts of both channels have now made it possible for me to see every Western ever made. The ones on ITV were best, because I could chase off in the commercials and break out a can of beans, but even with BBC I didn't risk missing much, since my husband can tell what will happen next in any Western within five seconds of switching it on, whether he's seen it before or not.

But we've never seen any film as constantly as *Butch Cassidy and the Sundance Kid*. I don't say *Gunsmoke* has been absolutely discontinued or that I've lost the power to spot when the girl must die (when she's engaged to the hero of a long-running serial like *High Chaparral*, that's when) or the gunwounds of a man prove fatal (when the actor's got a contract elsewhere, they will – as Robert Robinson says, when an actor wants to leave a series there's little that medical science can do). But all that has sunk into the background. What *is* it about this film?

I think I know, but to get the explanation you have to go

back a bit. The Western's original elements were pretty simple: man, horse, gun; territory without policemen; private matches played between good guys and bad guys (home) or Indians and the US Cavalry (away). Being a good shot and being in the right were supposed to go together, and you wore a white shirt to prove it. Realism was optional, John Ford as early as *Stagecoach* lovingly putting together the pieces of a vanished time, others simply filming endless footage – hoofage – of horses on the horizon and sticking them together as required.

As with all adventure stories it was the scenes that mattered, not the plot. Your great Western addict will recall the dying scene in *Gunfighter*, the tension mounting towards dark as they waited for the Indian attack in *The Searchers*, the moment in *Rio Bravo* where the villain hiding out in the room above reveals himself by dripping blood into the hero's beer. I wouldn't say when you've seen one Western you've seen the lot; but when you've seen the lot you get the feeling you've seen one – any able script-writer ought to be able to link *all* one's favourite scenes in the one scenario.

There was a pretty standard view of women. The tarty saloon girl might die saving the hero's life (as in *Destry Rides Again*) but never marry him; the cornfed heroine would probably get her man to say 'yes' in the end but that's about all he ever did say. John Wayne in *True Grit* pronounced his only believably sincere compliment when he said: 'She reminds me a lot of me.' Women might be useful to keep the plot going but they were not what it was all about: which was the construction and loving maintenance of a male ideal.

By the fifties people were beginning to play about more with the formula – the beauty of a pastoral convention, after all, is that you can stand it on its head or bounce ideas off it. *High Noon* (hero in *black* shirt) was supposedly about McCarthyism, *Red River* brought this business of the manly relationship to a really blushmaking point (and if Tito really sees it every other week he's got a cleaner mind than I have – or something). *Broken Arrow* and the like suggested that Indians (cf. Negroes) were human, too. *Duel in the Sun* very nearly did the same for women, though Gregory Peck's glamour never really suffered from treating the heroine like a saddlebag throughout.

Shane was supposed to mark the end of the gunfighter's day – but it did it with a bit of gunfighting for all that. For the one bit they couldn't change was the idea of a man proving himself by taking on death. 'One day,' a Quaker writer once said, 'I'll write a Western where the Quaker *doesn't* end up shooting somebody'; but I doubt if you could: the resolving gunshot is crucial. 'If Oedipus had been an American,' said Ronald Bryden, 'he'd have put someone else's eyes out' – being true to the code, of course.

And then came *The Wild Bunch*. I'm chary myself of violent anti-violence films – it's a bit too like *The People* denouncing vice (read all abaht it). But this really was the beastly film to end all beastly films. Not because the heroes were outlaws – so were Billy the Kid and Jesse James, in real life – but because its gang of gunfighters have all the riding, shooting outlaw camaraderie of the tradition – yet the whole thing is vile. In this one innocence doesn't save anybody – children burn insects for fun, bystanders are killed messily, for no point; the men don't have burly great hearts beneath their tough exteriors. I don't know if it's a film to convert you to pacifism, lesbianism or Communism, but it is the ultimate comeuppance of the he-male all-American free-shooting Western guy.

Well, we can't have *that*, for heaven's sake; Westerns are supposed to be fun. Morals are meant to help the myth along, not to make you sick to think of its implications. But ah! In the nick of time, there came Butch Cassidy to the rescue. About the same bunch – the Hole in the Wall gang – it is gay where the other was raw, stylish where the other was brutal, funny and with just enough apparent realism to satisfy the sophisticated seventies. *That's* better. We don't want no unpleasantness, boys, do we. When you call a man a butcher, *smile.*

What I Said Was . . . II

Get dressed now, Tom, will you? . . . Thomas, I asked you five minutes ago to GET DRESSED . . . TOM! Will you listen *when I speak to you – get your vest on at once, don't just stand there. . . .*

Ah, yes, he was always a dreamer, was our Tom . . . if he was thinking about something, it didn't matter what you said . . . lived in his imagination, even as a child. . . .

I suppose it would be too much to hope there was a clean shirt anywhere?

I just asked a simple question. I simply asked if there was a clean shirt, that's all. My God, can't I even *ask*?

Can't have that, now, can we, Mrs Muddlestone? Three weeks in arrears with the increase, that is. Well, you can start paying it off at 5s. extra on next week's rent, right?

I . . . I . . . well, Joe's been off . . . I'm not sure. . . .

. . . So I told him straight, I did. If you want the extra rent off me, I said, you'd best get them stairs fixed, I said. I said if you think we're going to live like pigs just so's you can have your fancy big car and a new pair of shoes every Tuesday you can just think again. I don't care, I said, you can do what you like. Two pound it is and two pound it's going to stay.

The Worry Ration

Last week I worried about the election and my son's football ankle. This week I'm worrying about money and rooms left empty for fear the tenants will be immovable. Next week it will be alcoholism and industrial unrest at Heathrow, the week after that the state of my coal cellar and recycling newspapers. The ration is two things a week and the rest will just have to take their turn.

Because honestly the thing is getting entirely out of hand. I think the moment when I drew up with a scream of hot rubber on tarmac was when we were all asked to worry a week or two ago about Sex for the Elderly. Tell me about spastics and I know I *ought* to provide money or attention even if I don't; the lonely plainly need visiting, distant floods require blankets and typhoid serum; if it's a political cause I could write to my MP; even with sex for the disabled I suppose they need us to push their wheel chairs closer together or something. But what in the name of heaven am I supposed to do about sex for the elderly?

Worry, that's all; how pointless. I know the theory is that concern for the frustrated, the aged or the forgotten Chinese children helps to change attitudes; to create at least a climate of opinion in which something might happen – double beds in the geriatric ward, maybe, or chow mein on the school dinner menus. But I wonder if it doesn't work the other way round as well.

When people discuss (and oh, brother, how they discuss) the sad, bad effects of television they don't just fasten on the purpose-built bashings and slashings; they wonder about the actual news itself. They point out that seeing so many tragedies you can't do anything about may, in the end, simply wear down the nerve ends so that there's no shock any more; you get too used to it, you just shrug. It could be that having our withers so constantly wrung on behalf of this or that distressed group, this aspect of the national disaster, that *piste* on the Gadarene slope has much the same effect: we get so that we hardly notice any of it.

We journalists may be largely to blame: we are but worriers for the working day, and get everybody het up about something which we then cheerfully forget on the Tube going home. But I fear the effect of our constant cries of woe may be a simple paralysis of the will; a weary impression that there are so many things we can't affect that it's pointless to try. 'Remember, Wormwood,' said demon Screwtape to his nephew the tempter, 'the more your man feels without acting, the less he will be able to act – and the less, in the long run, he will be able to feel.'

It's always the worry you can't do anything about that becomes a corrosive doomsday fantasy. Someone wrote to *The Times* once saying that it was all very well invoking the Dunkirk spirit, but at least during the war people were told what they should *do*: dig for victory, make do and mend, trap the germs by using your handkerchief; now the trouble is that we are always being told to prepare to meet our doom but not *how*. And in the current economic climate I would think this could be more important than it looks. For if, as I understand, the cash crises of capitalism are largely a matter of confidence (Roosevelt's 'we have nothing to fear but fear itself') then the more nervous everybody feels, the worse things actually will get. Whether we are told to buy now or buy later or buy British, whether we are supposed to be stocking up and bottling fruit, or patriotically not hoarding, whether we should be spending or saving or knitting mufflers for miners, I would have thought that *any* instructions, however chuckle-headed, would be better than none.

In the meantime, I'm dividing all causes, national and personal, into three groups. The ones I ought to do something about, and perhaps will; the ones I ought to do something about but know very well I won't; and the ones I know I can't do anything about at all and am going to stop thinking about. I may not succeed, but at least it's worth trying. Worry ought not to be used as in 'the mosquito worries the sunbather' but only, to my mind, as in 'the terrier worries the rat'.

Where the Money Goes I

This is the house that Jack built.
This is the farm attached to the house that Jack built.
This is the sty which cost so much it made a loss which recouped in tax the cost of the house that Jack built.
This is the pig that needed the sty that Jack built.
This is the swill they fed to the pig that lived in the sty that Jack built.
This is the bug that infested the swill that killed the pig and made *more* loss on the farm that Jack built.
This is the super de luxe all-in comprehensive water-softening system for the entire premises that prevented the bug that killed the pig that died in the sty that made the loss that recouped the cost of the farm and the house that Jack built....

The Fridge is Dead, Long Live the Fridge

My fridge has been declared legally dead. It shuffled off its mortal coil or something; the makers say it's past repair, but as they want £77 towards a replacement we're just learning to live with it. Each week it gives birth to an immense block of ice but, like the hospitals, we're getting better all the time at inducing delivery when it's convenient for *us*.

And it's funny what a much warmer, more personal relationship you have with a machine that only you can handle. Look at those clocks all over England that will only go on their sides, cisterns that will only fill if you hold down the ballcock with all the expertise of a poker-player raising on a busted flush; I suppose it gives you a feeling of power and involvement, like that egg you add to the cake mixes – just add kicks. And remember all those old films about India with railway engines snorting and spitting and refusing to move? The bunker-wallah who knew how to whack them into life was usually the cheeriest man in the movie.

Mind you, I wouldn't have taken so kindly to a fridge on borrowed time eight years ago. No, indeed. When you first move into a house everything is new, or you wish it was, and the slightest chip or hiccup in the pipes is an outrage: look how often you call round to admire someone's perfect new pad and find them in a state of hysteria about a slight crack at the back of the airing cupboard. They're quite right in a way, of course: for if ever they do stop fulminating, they'll go and get used to it; and it'll be there for ever.

We, for example, have this black plaster cherub (much disliked by our own white plaster cherubs) who lost a wing a while back; if we replaced it now he'd look as odd to us as the Venus de Milo with fresh arms. Again, my husband tried to take off the outer and uglier part of his lampshade; there was a blinding flash and a strong smell of burning author (Fahrenheit 459) and now all he has is two charred ends of flex. On his ceiling, I mean.

Is it just inertia that causes Beryl McAlhone, for example, to keep a superannuated piano in her garden? Or which inspired Honor Tracy's decaying Irish landowners not to bother with a new bell, just to put a trumpet by the door instead? I think it's rather that one feels more at home with these slightly collapsed objects. It's like shoes: you buy a new pair for their looks, but you go right on wearing the old ones because the holes that let the water in also let out the feet. There's comfort to an awful old dressing-gown a pretty peignoir is powerless to provide, and aging bra elastic is, I suspect, as near to liberation as most women ever get.

And I have a nasty feeling that much the same applies to people. Look at the savagery of early married rows: at that stage, imperfections in one's mate are intolerable, just like that crack at the back of the airing cupboard. Later, you just shrug: he only works on his side.

Newish friends, if they get ghastly, can be weighed and found wanting, but you'd never do a thing like that to old ones; their terrible habits are just part of the universe.

The chap who must absolutely be kept off the subject of the Pope after the third whisky; the people whose love-lives follow a sort of circadian rhythm, so that you can almost calculate when they'll be on the line in floods of tears again; the girl who, not content with just pressing a coin and a letter to post into the hands of a station porter, once actually filled his arms with paper, string, a pair of shoes and an address on an old bit of paper: none of these fuss me the way they would if they were colleagues or neighbours or *new* friends. I can never make out why in novels they sound so reproachful when they say 'You've changed!' Nobody I know, alas, ever does.

Maybe I'm exaggerating; maybe the second law of thermodynamics – the one about everything tending to collapse – hasn't actually got it in for me personally. But when you think how things fall apart ('The centre can't hold much longer, Cap'n!') it seems to me just as well that we meet their built-in obsolescence with our built-in indifference; that everything feels more normal when it isn't going pocketa-pocketa-pocketa according to plan; and that the dear old clothes we'll plainly be forced to wear for the next ten years are the ones we really love best anyway.

I've just realised I've talked myself into feeling rotten about my husband's mouldiest sweater. He says it's unfair that I told him it was unfit for wear but now keep wearing it myself. Doesn't he realise that we fridge midwives *need* something warm and comforting?

The T Factor

Hidden among the trees but not exactly covered by the Official Secrets Act, the Civil Service College at Sunningdale occasionally houses a seminar on communication between Government and people. I had always thought that the Civil Service used the word as in 'Communication Cord' – for emergencies only, £25 fine for improper use; so it was salutary to be reminded that they do, of course, have teeming departments to try to get things across to us.

But what puzzled me when I went to one of these seminars was the almost total neglect of what I had thought to be one of the main tools of government, the Tedium factor. Here were people talking about redesigning forms and simplifying posters and putting beef into their broadcasts; when I had always thought that boring the pants off the public was the normal way of catching it with its trousers down. True, most men at the top feel, as one put it, that '*all* communication is hostile to *all* government', but correct manipulation of the T-factor is surely the next best thing.

Take, for example, decimalisation. Did you really know what was going on until it was already too late? No doubt they told us – but how? Did you realise that those conversion tables sold in their thousands were no good except for thinking purposes, as they were accurate only to the nearest new halfpenny, and that the sums worked out in full came out quite differently? Did you know that from D-day all cheques would have to be in decimals, even if they're made out to a shop still using £sd? I bet you didn't – simply because the subject is so boring you've probably never read to the end of any paragraph about it. There was a vast explaining campaign after Christmas – but a lot too late to change anything.

The same with metrication. Half of us don't realise it's even threatening, the other half expected it to happen on 15 February with the decimals – both wrong. It's vaguely assumed to be coming, but there's been no bill through Parliament, no public row: no one's given it two minutes' thought except the professionals involved. Milk bottles will have to be remade for litres, which will give the dairies the excuse they've been longing for to use squeaky paper bags instead; the council will have to dispose of those and will put the rates up accordingly. We have had no serious say in any of it; yet I'm sure it's all there in the back pages of an HMSO publication somewhere.

I hesitate even to begin the next sentence, remembering Keith Waterhouse saying he could clear five million readers off the page with the single phrase 'Now about the Common Market . . .' but that, too, is a case in point. Polls, understandably not published, disclose 2 per cent for going in, 2 per cent for staying out and 96 per cent don't care—simply because the argument has been going on for 15 years and we're too tired to listen.

Even in detail the T-factor works: they go on and on and on about the price of butter (only that) till you think that if we all switched to Stork the problem would be over; if anyone ever took a different example we might sit up and say 'Hey, wait a minute . . .!' Internationalism has been so respectable for so long that no one seems to remember we may not get German efficiency, Italian flair and Danish design, so much as Swedish morals, Belgian clothes and Sicilian plumbing. We're like a parent who says to a child 'Oh do what you like but for pity's sake shut up', only to find he has given the child permission to put sand in the petrol tank.

Why are councillors reluctant to give their names? Because stories with names on them are interesting and get read. Why are White papers written on this crazed nineteenth-century assumption that any gentleman can write English as well as any other gentleman? Because if it's 300 pages long no one will read it anyway, and the whole battle can then be fought on the basis of judiciously worded handouts (better still, if you hold your press conference only 12 hours after releasing the thing: then no one *can* have read it).

What do you do if you have something you really want to get publicised, like 'Lost – Small Tabby Kitten' or 'Let-U-Down Minicabs'? You put stickers on lamp posts or cards through letterboxes. So when you have to announce that the area's to be redeveloped, what do you do? Print a small grey announcement in the local paper, naturally.

The world will end with a bang *and* a whimper, the whimper being the last politician saying, 'But we *told* you, in the footnote to paragraph 347 (F) (i) that in a non-negotiable situation our concept was to maximise the coefficient of escalation.'

The Real Thing

The man who hangs head downwards
Against the shaking sky
Reflects me in the water
And who he is or why
He knows no more than

I stir, he shifts beneath me
I halt, he stands stock still;
He knows not what constrains him
To move against his will
He only knows it ill.

And both will drown together
The mirrored man, and I
One falls, one rises upwards
To break the painted sky
But both of us will die

My father once presented this little-known piece of Housman to his class, and let several aficionados say how beautiful it was before he revealed that I had knocked it together with a history don in a bar. But what exact damage would he have done, I wonder, if he had let them think it was real?

It's a question one might well ask Elmyr de Hory, who has been described as the greatest faker of modern times. This man was a pupil of Léger, and says that Léger himself used to paint Corots in moments of financial strain; and that Vlaminck was once shown a row of Vlamincks and couldn't himself tell which were his own. It's a wise picture, even, that knows its own father.

Still, it's always a joy for the lay public to watch the art world tying itself in knots about 'derivative' works. First they thought Van Meegerens were Vermeers; then when he owned up they fell over themselves saying they had never believed it or, alternatively, m'lud, that the pictures were jolly good anyway. There was the fuss about the Holbein – *was* it any less likeable if it turned out not to be? And it's not only art, come to that: why should a man feel cheated if the bosom he caresses is stuffed with 58 per cent foam rubber – what's he after, its birth certificate? Herrick would have had a grievance if he'd had to rewrite his poem, 'Fair daffodils, we weep to see thee still bloody here at Christmas' – but if he hadn't *known* the daffodils were plastic?

There's the financial argument, obviously. If the X-ray shows that your Van Gogh was painted on a postwar sugar-sack marked Tate and Lyle, you won't get your money back – though if you only planned to keep it in a bank vault, that maybe serves you right. And if you ask why an absolutely perfect replica of a Georgian house shouldn't be as good as the original, the answer is that it's not just its looks you care about – you want the feel of Pope and Mozart in your bones.

Much the strongest argument against painted fakes is produced by the girl expert in Gavin Lyall's *Venus with Pistol* (*plug*) when she says, 'You don't buy a Poussin because you already know all about it, you buy because you *want* to understand. You want to sit and look and learn. And if it isn't a real Poussin you aren't learning.' Like the plastic/leather argument: the two bags may look the same the day you buy them, but the plastic will deteriorate while the leather weathers and grows.

But all this takes the traditional view: that art – or a book or a poem or whatever – as it were gives off something its creator put there, and it is up to us to get the message or not. However, plenty of painters and sculptors now take the line that it isn't 'what the artist is saying' that counts, but the inter-reaction between the work and the person looking at it. In that case you could still argue that the fake would not produce the inter-reaction – but supposing it did? Suppose, for example, that a de Hory 'Modigliani' did not have as much in it as one of Modigliani's Modiglianis but *for that reason* set up a better reaction with ignorant me? A book's abridged version may reach a child more easily; plenty of us understand bad French spoken by an Englishman better than the real thing.

Some modern artists might not even bother about forgery, money aside. You could hardly miss the touch of the artist's hand in something like Takis's ready-made light fittings. Jill Tweedie said recently that if 95 per cent of the inter-reaction was supplied by her beholding eye and only 5 per cent by the Andy Warhol exhibit, why didn't people buy her and not the picture? Indeed – and then would a fake Warhol be 95 per cent less heinous than a fake Leonardo as well as 95 per cent easier? Or it could be a matter of psychology, and whether you did better with a Canaletto or a Ganymede print of it would depend on whether you paid more attention if you thought it the original, or felt more at ease and receptive if you thought it a print.

Good heavens no, I can't answer these questions. But while you're on it, how about this one? You say something which I mishear as something funny. Whose crack is it? Not yours – you didn't say it. Not mine – I only heard it. Could it belong to the patron saint of faking, who cooks up one here and there just for laughs?

Travels with a Gin and Tonic

Cartier spent the winter of 1535 from November till April with his ships frozen into the ice, ravaged by scurvy and suffering from intense cold. Frank Pocock hobbled after Stanley on crutches, his feet lacerated with sores. One in six of the nineteenth-century emigrants to America died before they ever got there, of fights or disease in the stinking steerage . . . the men who have just got up Everest the hard way (as if there was an easy way, for heaven's sake) were bivouacking in conditions said to be like sleeping in a sheet sleeping bag in a deep freeze.

There's been a boom in perfectly awful adventure. A BBC series on the explorers, each more wretched than the last; a new edition of *Alive*, the account of the footballers who survived for two months after their plane crashed in the high Andes; there's a beautiful new *Atlas of Exploration* from Mitchell Beazley; we can settle down any evening to the horror of the Donner expedition, say, which took the wrong turning in the great salt desert and had to overwinter in terrible cold with nothing to eat but each other; or Barents building his driftwood house (that was not discovered again for 300 years) only to die seven days after they set off again in the spring; or Darwin in the *Beagle* taking a month against mountainous seas even in midsummer to battle his way to the ghastly Tierra del Fuego.

What they got out of it was one thing – excitement, gold, glory, the lure of the unknown, a tomb in Westminster Abbey. But what do we get out of it? Not the lure of the unknown, certainly – not when you know that all the Donner expedition paved the way for was Joe's Diner on Route 40 across Utah.

It would be pleasant to think that we're getting inspiration, that all this will stir us into meaningful effort in the hour of national crisis, etc., etc.

But do we really feel the urge to grab alpenstock and tent, boot and gun, to rush out into the trackless waste? Well, I don't know about you, but what I feel is exactly the opposite. Amundsen blew the gaff when he said that he was attracted by the suffering of the great explorers; so am I, so am I – because it's so splendid that it isn't happening to me.

Nothing makes the bedclothes seem warmer than all that frostbite at 60°C below; nothing puts zip into the fish fingers like reading about the weevilly flour and the diseased wallabies (that was Giles in the Australian desert). There may be a couple of things wrong with our times, but a few refreshing moments contemplating the Navy in the eighteenth century will make it seem a paradise – there's a picture of The Death Ship in the World Atlas showing that only 8·3 per cent of the wretched tars died by enemy action – disease took half of them and accident, fire, sinking and wreck took care of the rest.

And if you keep your mind solidly fixed on the slave ships of the eighteenth century and what it must have been like in a wooden vessel becalmed in the tropics for weeks on end, even air travel seems luxurious.

Of course this is not an emotion one is really supposed to have – we were all taught to tut-tut in school at the thought of the blessed at the bar of heaven getting any sort of kick out of the writhings in hell beneath them. But there it is, we do.

For full enjoyment, the miseries have to be over and done with – we may not in practise be able to do a thing about Bangladesh or Chad or the way Americans treat their old folk, but we do feel we *ought* to be doing something; it would be inhuman to get any sort of bang out of real (i.e., contemporary) suffering. And the rules of the game dictate that no one shall actually be tortured, raped, flayed or impaled to any great extent. Human beings presumably do enjoy hearing about such things if the Aztec executions or the box office of *Straw Dogs* are anything to go by, but these are forbidden and repulsive emotions, in no way to be compared with the way you can sink into a warm bath all the more cheerfully for reading about all those poor bleeders without boots in the Crimea. Which is why I have by my bed two engravings of some wretches being awfully cold in boats; it's as good as a hot-water bottle on a chilly evening.

The 'Explorers' series tonight is to give us Burke and the Australian desert. A pity; I prefer my explorers cold, at least in wet weather. Never mind, I daresay they'll have a perfectly horrible time of it in one way or another.

Yes please, ice and lemon with it, and would you mind passing me that cushion.

Home and Away

The white house glimmers through
the trees;
The grave and gentle candles shine.
'Here, surely, here at last is peace' . . .
Perhaps he thinks the same of mine.

I doubt it, actually, since those who stay in my house, with or without me around, tend to complain a good deal about things which don't bother me in the least, like the fridge door not opening. But a golden glow does seem to hang over the houses I visit; bald envy leaves me with a considerable re-entry problem into my own, and a depressing conviction that there's almost no place like home, dammit.

How do they do it, I keep asking myself: superior meals apparently produced on half an hour's work a day, decors in which nothing is out of place? And my hostesses, on the principle of setting the peasantry at ease by spilling red wine on the snowy cloth themselves, even manage to arrange that one of *their* children has an hour-long tantrum first. I know perfectly well that other people, too, can clear up for company, but there are tell-tale signs of a really ordered life. Sooner or later every visitor walks into a cupboard in mistake for a room, and either is or isn't showered with fir-cones and old ping-pong nets. And however much of a spurt you put on, it could never reach the scaley bottom of the children's tooth-mug.

Of course (I tell myself) one does take other people's arrangements at face value. If there's a lump of rock on your own floor, you start hunting the blood of the clot who brought it in; on someone else's you assume it's a doorstop. In your own house you're uneasily aware of all the hidden bodies (summer dinner parties are hell because you can't stuff things behind the curtains). In other people's you see the surface: I'd admired a friend's round tables with floor-length cloths for years before she mentioned that they were only plywood rickracks, not proper tables at all. Just as sociologists always seem to describe other cultures as 'the way they cope' and their own as 'the way our arrangements break down', so you always assume that the things you see in other people's houses must be *meant*.

Other people's priorities show up particularly well in holiday houses. I stayed last year with a family whose appealing principle was to collapse completely on inessentials like bedtimes and polished silver and the guinea-pig straw. On the other hand, the children were *never* allowed in a boat without lifejackets, and there was not one but two vast tanks of hot water for those baths which alone make Suffolk an inhabitable county. And there was the curious lady who made splendid meals in her little French hovel to the strains of Vivaldi – it was a shock to realise they had been 'converting' this untended pile not for six months but for six years; that they got the electricity for the stereo long before there was any sort of substitute for an Elsan.

At least, you think, you can filch some bright ideas from other houses. One woman I know has not a bucket, but a whole dustbin under the sink, lined with its plastic bag – and another has the same, but with a flap for shoving in gunk with one hand. One house has a bulletin board in the lavatory, the one place it can't be missed; in another they just write messages on the bathroom mirror with a lipstick. I have one friend of the irritating sort who picks up antique tables for 50p; instead of then paying £50 for three months' hard for french polishing, she tops them with a carefully cut circle of Formica.

From a single hostess I gleaned the idea of a curtain rail above the work surface, the bashers and scoopers depending therefrom on hooks; of a set of leather-lidded boxes to put things in which would need far less shifting of people and papers than the ordinary storage chest; and of the one-plant-wide flower bed, which surely even I could keep in order. That one, whose children line up of a morning to receive cards with their day's chores upon them, has solved the problem of the square-eyed child sitting too close to the TV: it's up on the wall in a corner, as in a pub. And I have suddenly realised what, in any house, distinguishes the ornaments from the mess – no mean feat, when anything from a clockwork mouse to a pair of Victorian eyebrow-tweezers just might be there for decoration. If the space on each side of it is symmetrically equal, then it's an ornament.

You come home full of such good resolution: your children too, are going to cook lunch, your flower vases sport dried grasses, your husband build a gazebo in the garden. But it doesn't work, of course. For one thing, you haven't trained your children to be cooks or your husband to be Nash. But the more serious reason is that, when all's said and done, your own compromise is your own compromise: you can't have both the icy perfection of Kate's acres of laminate *and* the dark grotto of Elizabeth's cassoulet corner; you can hardly achieve both the bold gaiety of X's free-range children and the merciful silence of Y's battery-bred.

And after a few days one stops seeing those disenchanting damp patches on the basement wall and unread piles of *New Society;* you hardly even notice as you knock into the camera equipment for the fortieth time. You slip back; and all is well again.

Until, of course, someone threatens to come to stay.

A Vet's Life

'Of course I've done snakes!' said the vet. 'Good heavens, I'm an honorary member of half the strip clubs in London.' The girls do suggestive things with snakes, it seems, and when the snake gets sick, there goes Mr Giles, little black bag in hand, to stiffen it up: 'and it isn't easy, in a tiny dressing-room, with a great pink bottom two inches from your ear and somebody trying to stick feathers on to it'.

I'd no idea a vet's life could be so testing. You don't get much inkling of all that, sitting in the waiting-room reading *Will your bitch come on heat and spoil your plans?* for the fortieth time. You can study the other suppliants, of course, as in an agent's waiting-room: the theatrical bitch with trailing dugs hamming it up with one limp paw – 'she's got a terrier friend in the country, she digs the hole, he chases the rabbits. . . . ' With one paw, she digs – and naturally has lacerated toenails as a result. And there are always a fair sprinkling of sixtyish women who have managed to get their hair the same colour as their pets.

'Ah, I like this one,' said Giles as the first patient came into the surgery. 'He's a very enthusiastic working dog.' The very enthusiastic dog glowered from the door: he'd plunged through a thorny hedge and had a bad eye. Once on the table, however, he gazed upwards with that air of martyrdom that spaniels do so well and received cream into it.

'Eating all right?'

'Oh, God yes.' An injection; out they went. Cats and dogs were about balanced that morning; and there were no oddities. It's the wrong time of year for tortoises – they only happen in spring when you are trying to get them to wake up. And no goldfish – but do you know how you give medicine to a goldfish? Put it in the water. Imagine if the children had to swim in their rose-hip syrup. Mostly the creatures got injected: 'If I give them pills, the owners don't like to admit it if they can't get the pills into them,' Giles explained – and I took his point, remembering how he and my husband had once spent twenty solid minutes trying to get a pill into one of our cats, ending up with six scratches, two whiskies and a firm conviction that the cat could do without.

In fact, I was a bit shaken to see the sedate procession of well-controlled animals who loped in, mounted the table, jumped down in good order; I had assumed that others, too, had to grapple their animals on to the table and then sink down to table height when they took refuge on the head. 'And they don't fight out there, either,' said Giles. 'It's like the behaviour of some animals at a water-hole.'

As surgery ended, the X-ray machine arrived. 'This is where we give the lie to the idea that dogs eat bones,' groaned Mr Peters, the other partner, as they heaved a blocked dog on to the table. Would the log-jam within yield to flooding from below? The X-ray showed it would. 'Now get that door open and belt out there with the dog as soon as I say,' said Peters. 'To the street?' 'No, you get fined £20 for nuisance out there – and I don't suppose we could chalk it up to publicity. *Now*.' With the smoothness of a waiter decorking champagne, they whipped out the enema, tamped a swab on the dog and ran. I let myself off looking out into the yard.

Upstairs they have a little operating theatre: a Lakeland terrier was lying limp, having some extra inbred teeth removed from 'its silly little deformed mouth'. Did they operate on birds? 'Yes,' they said, 'but pretty silly it looks, a budgerigar on that vast table fixed up to the anaesthetic'. Outside there were diverse cats greyly recovering from their Goodbye to All That. 'People have the most extraordinary views on their cats' sex-life,' marvelled Giles. Very permissive girls hate the thought of limiting their cats' fun, and some ladies are over keen the other way round. Though Giles thinks there is a case for this: there's a cat colony on a hospital building site nearby where a Royal Free time is had by all; the trouble is, they don't get enough to eat, they've got endemic cat flu, and when they despoil the builders' materials they are apt to sustain a half-brick in the stomach. It takes a Mehitabel to get much fun out of a life like that.

After that, out on the rounds. Giles had once been flown to Austria to do a hysterectomy on Lord Birley's St Bernard, and now another Birley bitch was in trouble, in the old-fashioned sense – on account of the dashing Jack Russell next door, whose pups she was too small to bear. An injection. Then a pale whippet that matched the rich curtains, for inspection; on to a retriever in a fancy flat, with whom Giles instantly raced to the kitchen. 'She gets so emotional when she sees me, she pees,' he explained, as they mopped the lino. And we plunged upstairs through a busy pub to attend a couple of gingery corgis: one of them, with a face like a fox and a body like a bagwash, had been bitten in the rump by the other. It reminded me of an anti-monarchist I'd met once: his whole political case was that the Queen had taught people to think that corgis were nice.

A full morning's work, indeed; no wonder the poor man turned pale at lunch when his grouse was badly underdone; he hardly knew whether to eat it or cure it. After that, I didn't have the heart to ask him my last question: about a cockatoo called Beauty (I swear this is true) who went bald when her first owner, a stripper, bathed her in detergent. Was she wise, I wondered, to try to restore her feathers by faith-healing?

Keeping Cool

This is just a short message of cheer for those of you who are reading this column mainly in order to put off getting on with the Christmas cards. And the message is this: not only is it not too late for whatever you haven't got around to doing, but it is quite possibly too early.

For there are only two ways of avoiding an absurd fuss about events like Christmas and birthdays and the arrival of cousins from Australia: and you've missed the first anyway. This is the system used by an aunt of mine whom we will call Oriana the Organised. All aunts are organised, but she is in a class by herself: a week before a holiday she was complaining she hadn't a thing to wear – because all her pretty dresses were already packed. Presumably the first mandarin to start the habit of putting down eggs for future generations thought he was just being a little forehanded with the breakfast. Such people doubtless bought their Christmas crackers in the July sales, will be making next year's Christmas cake this weekend and have already bought their New Year Alka-Seltzer; the hell with them.

But for those of us who are not usually organised enough even to cut the toenails on both feet on the same evening, any attempt to get a bit ahead is likely to make things even worse. If we started our shopping three weeks ago, that doesn't mean it's over now, it just means we've been bothered about it for three weeks already. All we ever succeed in doing is spreading out the agony, like the fools who have one tooth filled every Monday for a month, or those who drive five hours a day for five days instead of belting for two and basking for the last three. No wonder we pronounce 'season's greetings' in Scottish – as in 'dinna greet, ma wee bairn'.

No; the only way to cut down on the fuss is to hack away at it from the other end; to wait longer and longer before you bestir yourself at all. For Christmas, like packing and homework, takes as long as you've got. Especially the entertaining: two weeks ago I had some people coming, and what with one thing and another I hadn't even bought the food by lunchtime. Naturally both I and my trembling family expected the tail-spin of all time to follow – but somehow it didn't happen.

Quite a few other things didn't happen either, as a matter of fact, like the salad, and getting the mess off the stairs. But nobody seemed to mind; and the fact that we weren't eating the kind of food it takes days to prepare meant that, in the words of Monica Dickens, 'everything went right, it was most extraordinary'. I learned an elementary Parkinsonian lesson: that no fuss can be greater than the time between its beginning and its object.

Leave it, leave it; there's time enough. All right, so you didn't post early for Christmas – they trail around with half-empty sacks the last three days, anyway. So you won't have time to clear up – just dump some holly on top, it'll look all right. The shops, agreed, will be jammed with last-minute panickers for the next four days – very well then, do what Paul Jennings does, and shop airily just before the shops shut on Christmas Eve; he even claims he has got discounts from assistants giggly with their Christmas sherry. And if anybody tries to get severe with you, you just tell them that a perfectly managed Christmas correct in every detail is, like basted inside seams and letters answered by return, a sure sign of someone who hasn't enough to do.

Baby Talk

Not you, of course. You think before you speak, you do. Of course you wouldn't make a nasty remark about someone else's gammy leg; what an idea. And naturally you're dead against pollution and very concerned about the future of the planet. So it isn't you that's been going around saying, 'When are you going to start a family?' 'Isn't your daughter expecting yet?' 'Don't want to leave it too long you know.' Or even, in that very careful tone which isn't much more obvious than an elephant falling through a fourth-floor skylight, '*Are* you going to have children, do you think?'

Still, plenty of people have been saying these things – even to a girl I know who is still in her twenties, has only been married four years, and, with dodgy health and a husband about to change jobs, has excellent reasons for waiting. And I bet half of them aren't remotely conscious of being even tactless let alone anti-social. Which just means they haven't thought about it.

Any married couple without children is in one of three states. Either they're trying to produce some and can't, in which case these needling little questions are about as kindly as asking a cripple why he isn't running in the school sports. Or they're undecided. If so, enough of such snide cracks just might push them into it – thus distorting a decision people surely ought to make with their eyes open, and maybe leaving one of them feeling they were bounced into it all too soon.

Or the couple actually don't want any children. In which case, what the hell do these maternal ladies think they're doing? We have masses of TV and newspaper space devoted to the population problem; not a soul but thinks we have to do something about it; if ever there's to be a family of more than 1·2 again *somebody*'s got to lay off, to right the balance. But what hope do we have of ever curbing the world's fertility at all, if even in the educated sections of an advanced country a woman can't abstain without being made to feel a freak? And that's exactly what such chat can do. I remember trying to get a group of rather shy Kenyan women talking and the great common topic turned out to be babies; after two hours of 'When my seventh was weaned, I . . .' and 'You had a dreadful time with your fifth didn't you?' I felt positively *empty*.

People might be a little less glib in their recommendations, I think, if they took a closer look at their real motives for making these cracks. For it's not, I'm convinced, that they're really so upset at the thought of their dear friends missing out on the blessings of motherhood; on the contrary. Who's she, your primeval subconscious is saying to you, to get out of being chained to the house for weeks on end – up in the night with bottles and ear-oil – giving up trips to the hairdresser for the sake of trips to the zoo? And if the childless couple aren't quite so hard up as everyone else because of it, then heaven help them. I know a successful novelist who is childless because years ago she conceived in the Fallopian tube and was very lucky not to die of it; for 25 years she's had to put up with people saying she has 'chosen material success' instead of self-sacrificing parenthood.

And everybody had darned well better know how self-sacrificing they are, these mothers. A pregnant friend of mine squeezed behind the lunch table the other day for a cosy chat about the forthcoming event; she said the trouble with pregnancy was not so much the morning sickness, or being unable to get through turnstiles, but the advice you had to endure. She was amazed at the Just You Wait attitude of so many women, who told her to wash her own nappies with her own hands lest they be not white enough, who dwelt gloatingly on the loss of freedom; 'And all these fantastic little bootees and bonnets and things – *are* they really necessary?' Well, of course not; but how can you say in later life After All I've Done for You, unless you've always been clearly prepared to fuss, fuss and fuss again?

Almost all the really nasty tribal rituals concerned with reproduction, like slicing off a girl's genitalia in Somaliland or making a baby catch its death 'waiting naked for God' at Breton christenings, are enforced not by male chauvinist pigs but by female chauvinist sows who don't see why these young girls should get away with having an easier time than they had. There's a strong masochistic streak in women which makes them feel not only that the common lot of women is pretty bloody, but that it somehow ought to be.

The family planners are puzzled that today's young woman, far from spacing her family, as was the original idea, gives birth like a pop-up toaster. Is she trying to get it all over in one fell swoop (which doesn't suggest she enjoys it all that much) or subconsciously feeling that if you don't suffer like a hag-ridden Victorian, you aren't really doing your stuff?

Perhaps what we should do is to play up the frightfulness of the working life, chained to a hot typewriter all day – changing the boss's paper napkins almost hourly – pushing the car for miles because of the noise it's making, just like a yowling pramful. For if we could once get rid (however wrongly) of the idea that you can actually have a good life without children, then – just possibly – the good women would leave alone those very very few who are not contributing to the population problem.

Job Lot

Did Metternich, one asks oneself, ever break off at the Congress of Vienna to persuade the Spanish Ambassador that he wanted a ginger kitten? Did Leonardo have to cut short the day's session on the Madonna of the Rocks to get a birthday parcel to the post office on time? Did Palmerston ever have to hurry home from the Foreign office because the builder was expected hourly? I doubt it.

All the arguments about women keeping up with men focus on the large areas – what they are going to do about their children, their temperament, the meals and the cleaning. What no one allows for, and what really hobbles us in the race, is the incredible amount of little extra jobs that no amount of professional commitment can get you out of – not if you're a woman.

Take birthdays. A few men are good at birthdays, most not; but it's always the woman who finally has to remember the far-flung uncle, come up with some pretty paper and string, find the blasted card. And once you start adding in the time taken to get child A organised to give a present to child B, and the cake and the party and the balloons, you can write off a couple of weeks a year for it. No way of streamlining it, either; you can bulk-buy cards and paper, I suppose, but you can hardly buy thirty breadbins for the whole crew – can't afford it, nowhere to keep them, and who knows what they'll want in September, anyway?

Or these wretched pets. All right, no one has to have kittens, as I keep telling the cat; but no matter whose animal it technically is, who ends up taking it to the vet to have its hernia fixed? (How does a kitten *get* a hernia, anyway – they don't lift many heavy weights.) However liberated the family, however the work is shared, no one ever seriously expects the man of the house to be the one to do something about the scaly patch on the back of the guinea-pig.

Anyone who comes to a house, too, is automatically supposed to be something the wife should have seen to. My husband's grievance of the week is having been roused in quick succession by a window-cleaner (who knows when a window-cleaner, any more than lightning, will strike?), a needy knifegrinder and a man asking him to move the car because they were laying on a water supply for the vicar – and making about as much mess as if he were having it piped from the Jordan River. By what conceivable stretch of imagination is moving the car for the roadmen women's work? But you don't have to stretch your imagination; you just have to remember that women are the residual legatees of all odd jobs whatsoever. This is the missing element in all those silly calculations where one journalist says that a woman's work is worth 428·82½p at the going rate; and another says, no it's not, not when you've deducted tax, stamp and payment for a man's work in tool shed and garage.

Another thing one never allows for is other people's troubles. A friend rings you up because her daughter's on pot or her husband's left; you want to hear about it, you are all for the endless telephone calls, the come-round-at-once; but you forget, brutal though it sounds, that sympathy takes time as well as tea. And any woman who calmly opted out of that wouldn't be professional, she'd be plain inhuman.

And that goes, too, for a lot of footles round the neighbourhood. Men aren't bad at Action Groups, when there's a threat to property; but when it comes to sales of work, PTA, taking your lollipop turn at the crossing, trudging round to see the aged – that's for the birds. And if you do manœuvre your man into going, say, to hear about reading methods in the school, he comes back disgusted: he could have read all that in a book, all they really wanted him to do was Participate; participation is the thief of time; it's ridiculous.

I'm not saying men can't be sympathetic – sometimes. They do feel a sense of local obligation – occasionally. But a man who opts out of helping or sick-visiting or thank-you letters gets away with it. I don't know why we so readily assume men have a shallower sense of obligation – they are, after all, God's creatures – I'm not even sure it isn't vaguely insulting. But there it is: if something's got to be done, the chances are that it's a woman – and a busy one – who will sigh and do it.

The only consolation is that in the long run we score: the person with too much to do always gains over the person with too little. At least when a woman retires, in so far as she ever does, it's not the total cut-off that can leave a man with nothing to do all day but sit in front of the TV twiddling the knobs. Only I just wish, when neither of us has written to my husband's mother, I didn't feel so much worse about it than he does.

Who's Having Kittens?

We think it's time Mark had a pet of his own, so we're letting him keep one of the kittens – he's called it Mog. I suppose three cats *is* rather much, but Simon and I believe in having animal families around – it's the obvious way of learning the Facts and all that, don't you think? Then they don't have to get it all off lavatory walls, or read those speechlessly earnest little books; they just see how naturally it all happens to the animals.

Oh, look, Mark, there's Mog's father at the window – isn't that nice, he's come to see her. Yes, I'm sure it's her father – he's ginger, and she's got a lot of ginger in her fur. No, Paddy isn't her father. I know he's black and there's black in her fur too, but he can't be.

He just *can't* be, that's all.

Well, look, let me explain. Long, long ago poor Paddy had to have an operation, and since then he hasn't been able to – well, to have any kittens. Sometimes they have to do that to cats, if they live in high flats and can't get out, for example. Gracious no, of course they don't do it to people. I don't care what Daddy said about Mr Heath's Cabinet, that was a *joke*.

Shut the window, for heaven's sake, there's that ginger tom again. Yes, I know he's her father, but he can't come in. Not now. Well, he might come in and – and eat her food. D*on't* let her out! I *know* she's crying to be let out, that's just the point. Well, lady cats just do make that noise sometimes.

Because they – well, when a lady cat wants to find a mate – that's the same as a husband – and start having little kittens, then she makes that noise. No, of course I didn't – I couldn't make that noise if I tried. No, I will *not*.

Well, usually when a cat feels like that, she goes out at night, you see, and it's dark, and she has to make a special noise so that all the male cats will hear her and know to come and mate with her . . . no, well, cats can have several husbands, it's not quite like people. Oh, for God's sake, Simon, don't make it any *more* difficult – I'm trying to explain this sensibly, leave the Smiths out of it. Lady cats mate with several tomcats, and then when the seed has found the egg the little kittens will grow inside her tummy, and then after nine weeks they'll come out, just as you came out of my tummy. All right?

Oh, Mark, you've let her out! I *told* you! Well, yes, I know it's only her father, but you see cats don't always understand that, I mean Mog doesn't *know* it's her father, it's different with people. Well, it may have happened once in the Bible, but that was a long time ago. Of course I know about Lot, but you don't want to believe everything some wretched little church-goer tells you.

Hell, that son-of-a-bitch has got into the jigsaw cupboard and kicked the whole lot out. . . . What? A bitch is a lady dog. No, I don't mean really, of course she came from another cat. I know she isn't a dog, it's just a way of saying something rude about someone. Well, I suppose not everyone does like puppies, that's all.

I expect she was looking for a place to have her kittens. Mummies do the same sort of thing, they make the house nice and clean to have a good place for their babies to be born. You could find a box for her and put something soft in it – no, *not* your school sweater – for her to have her kittens on. When we've cleared up all this jigsaw. After all, she is your cat.

Darling, I'm so sorry she scratched you – I suppose she was frightened to have you come too close. Well, I know you watched a cat have kittens on school television but that was different – it wasn't people near the poor cat, it was just a camera. Well, then, that's one of the facts they jolly well should have told you: cats like to be left alone. No, I wasn't, because I had you in hospital – Daddy at first, and then a nurse and the doctor – Mog doesn't need a doctor, she can do it all herself – look, she's licking them clean now. Oh for *heavens sake*, Mark, what a disgusting idea. Can't you get it into your head that she's a cat, she's not a person? She's *different*.

Social Words for Social Workers I

Suggestive Results: Those based on a survey of twenty-three handpicked persons in a university town. The phrase enables those who have not the resources or the patience to slog away at a real survey to go ahead and make generalisations anyway.

Ego differentiation: Knowing where you leave off and the client begins; important because if you begin, client is likely to leave off.

Empire building: Attempt by another social worker to get enough staff.

Necessary Expansion of department to deal with increased case load: Attempt by oneself to get enough staff.

Consensus work: Usually futile effort to get a group to work together – successful mainly with tenants' associations, squatters, and small gangs who are good at beating up other gangs.

Ancient, Liberal, Humane

My father and I arrived in Athens together; but I doubt if we saw the same city. I saw the stucco of the airport, the blue-chinned official leafing through his grubby black-list; the hot streets choked with petrol fumes and the widening sprawl of the modern town – an Athens run at that point with the jack-boot illiberalism of a tenth-rate banana republic. He saw the Athens of the 5th century BC.

To him, the real Greece was the one whose marble bones stick up through the soil of time, the Greek running through his head the Greek of Homer and Euripides and Plato, not the starling clatter of the present day. And if you asked him about the city, he would remember the statesman Pericles, who said of it in 431 BC: 'Our constitution is called a democracy because power is in the hands not of a minority but of the whole people. When it is a question of settling private disputes everyone is equal before the law . . . no one is kept in political obscurity by his poverty. . . . Our love of what is beautiful does not lead to extravagance; our love of the things of the mind does not make us soft. . . .' To stand on the Acropolis when we went was the supreme irony: in the city that gave us the standards by which we judge the Colonels, to stand among the ruins of democracy.

My father has taught Greek and Latin for fifty years; but I was touched only by the fringes of it. I could see the endless procession of Old Boys trotting back in gratitude ten, twenty, forty years on. I heard how he surprised his colleagues by using the set vocabulary, but not in the set fashion, so that the boys, instead of ploddingly translating 'It is pleasant in summer to swim in the sea' or 'Old men are wise', found themselves construing 'It is pleasant in summer to chase old men into the sea'. His yellowing photograph of the Demeter of Cnidos, his little statue of Socrates, the sceptical snort with which, throughout my childhood, he greeted the pronouncements of the Government, the weather forecaster and the Archbishop of Canterbury – all this was obvious enough; but not being a classicist myself I never got to the heart of the matter. This spring journey was a pilgrimage: to go back to the source of it all and find out, if I could, what he was all about – what it was about the classics, and especially Greece, that has given the world so much.

Walking with him among the stumps of stone, looking up at the restored glory of the Parthenon, I could begin to imagine what this place must have once been like; but the amazement remained. How could anyone have an eye so exact that he would raise the floor of the Parthenon by 4⅝ inches over a span of 76 yards to correct an optical illusion? How on earth could this people, a couple of centuries away from dummylike religious idols, have made marble figures so perfect that you feel you could peel the fabric off the thighs and breasts and ankles and find the real thing underneath?

This city saw the start of our philosophy – everyone begins with Plato; of our mathematics – Pythagoras worked out the maths of the musical scale, even; of our drama – the tragic figures of Oedipus and Antigone, Orestes and Electra haunt us still. And all in a remarkably short span of time. Almost all that we remember was sandwiched roughly between the defeat of the Persians at Marathon in 490 BC (we get our word from the efforts of the man who ran twenty miles to gasp out the good news in Athens) and the arrival of Philip of Macedon in 340 BC. Yet enough went on in those years to set our standard still: a tremendous boiling up of every sort of involvement. Poets competed in the games, mathematicians were also philosophers; if there was a war to be fought they all fought it; and everybody but everybody was mixed up in politics. Their democracy was dauntingly total. Their officials were chosen by lot, and they took it in turns to be chairman; so that anybody could find himself, for one day, the man who signed for the city.

As in any other democracy, you could have a persuasive leader like Pericles; but he wasn't a ruler, and they didn't have what my father calls 'the cheerful way the other city states had of putting their political rivals to death'. In the case of a political deadlock between two points of view, they had a civilised system from which we get our word ostracise: everyone voted, by writing a name on a bit of pot or *ostrakon*, to banish with full honours one of the two contenders for ten years. Once the quarrel was between Themistocles, who wanted to build up the navy, and Aristides the Just, who favoured the soldiers on land; a peasant asked Aristides to help him mark an *ostrakon* against him. 'But why?' asked Aristides. 'I've nothing against him,' said the peasant, 'I'm just so sick of hearing him called "The Just".'

They had an equivalent of the House of Lords, the Areopagus, but as democracy grew stronger, its power declined. 'It's the same pattern in all these things,' my father explained. 'The first row is always between the new commercial class and the old landowners who don't understand trade and don't like it; the powerless proletariat can't do anything without a leader. It's often a disgruntled aristocrat who starts a revolution, gets a bodyguard and enthrones himself, and sits firmly on the heads of the old landowners. He'll probably do things to educate the proletariat, and then when they get fed up and chuck him out they're sufficiently mature to run things themselves.'

Athenian democracy didn't go so far as to include such riff-raff as women or captured foreign slaves, but perhaps that was a bit much to expect: no one but the Greeks, after all, had even heard of the idea of democracy. The other city states veered between democracy and oligarchy: only Sparta never even tried democracy. They had two kings (like two shirts, 'one to wash the other . . .'), and having conquered most of the southern part of the Peloponnese spent so much time trying to hold down their slave population that they never had any left over for poetry or philosophy.

My father's love of Athens was plainly only equalled by his loathing for Sparta. 'Boneheaded Spartans,' he would say, 'good old public school OTC militarists; all they could do was get in a line and push; and if anyone tried anything different they said it wasn't cricket. There was an intelligent Theban once – they only ever had two – called Epaminondas; he put his stronger forces not on the right of the battle like everyone else but on the left, so they fought the Spartan crack troops and beat them; Epaminondas's rabbits never had to bat at all. The Spartans were most indignant – and they fell for exactly the same trick nine years later.'

My father snorted. 'All that business of the mothers telling their sons: "Come back with your shield or on it" – perfectly stupid, if you've got to retreat you'd much better throw away your shield; it's too heavy.'

I asked about the Spartans' heroism at Thermopylae, where 300 of them defended a narrow pass against the Persians and all but one of them died. One is often told the story as if they knew they were doomed when the battle began, but others, my father included, think not: 'It was a last desperate attempt to jam the enveloping army between two wings of the Spartan forces and it didn't come off; not even a Spartan would be so stupid as simply to sit down and say "We will now die".'

Apart from the Persians, there were two things that linked the city states: the Gods, and the Games. Not just the Olympic games, but a good many others; and not just the athletics, either. We know all about the runners and charioteers and the victor's crown of leaves; what gets forgotten is that contests in poetry and playwriting were important too. You get some feeling of what the plays must have been like, sitting among the pines and olive trees in a theatre like Epidaurus, a perfect surviving example of the Greek theatre – perfect, that is, except for the inevitable German reciting Schiller in the middle. We got rid of her at last and I made my father recite some Greek instead – he dropped a sixpence on the central stone and it rang with absolute clarity right up to the back row where I was sitting. He used to make his pupils learn Greek (and Latin, and English) poetry by heart; they always complained at the time but thanked him later – none more keenly than one who was aide de camp during the war to Air Marshal Garrod when they liberated Athens, and Garrod made him stand in the centre of the theatre of Dionysus and recite a huge slab of the Antigone.

The audience of ancient Greece knew all the myths on which the plays were based; there wasn't any action because it all happened off stage; there's no avoiding the conclusion that they sat on those excruciating stone seats simply to listen to the music and the words. From there they would have seen the great doors close as Clytemnaestra went in to kill Agamemnon, seen them open as Oedipus, knowing at last that he is his father's killer and his mother's man, groped his way forward without his eyes. There they would have heard the classic argument between Antigone, who insists on burying her brother according to the law of the gods, and her sister Ismene who is horrified at disobeying their uncle who has forbidden it: 'Ismene has a sentence I always used on my victims,' my father remembered. 'She says "I am constitutionally incapable of going against public opinion" – that's you lot, I used to tell them.' Antigone knows what she must do and Antigone dies.

The conflict between private and public conscience, in that play, between the law of vengeance and a duty to one's mother, as in the Electra, between what you plan to do and what fate seems to have in store for you – the questions and the myths have obsessed the world ever since, from Eliot to Anouilh and a dozen lousy film directors, from Byron to Cocteau, to the psychologists, to W. B. Yeats.

Yet they were myths, even then, to the Greeks; and in one respect we have the edge on them, for we have seen Mycenae. Even a hundred years ago Agamemnon and Menelaus and Odysseus and the whole Trojan war were thought to be legends – until a determined little Austrian named Schliemann passionately dug up first Mycenae and then Troy itself. Then the towering figures of the warriors were seen for what they were: the Acheans, the first Greeks of all. Everything about them was larger than life: they swept down from the mountains of central Europe; they reached as far as Crete; they took up the delicate civilisation of the Minoans, those people excellent at plumbing and painting, whose golden bull led to the legend of the Minotaur; whose civilisation was linked with the city that blew up on Santorin and may have been the lost Atlantis.

The Acheans built with stones too colossal, it seems, to be moved by any human being: their walls at Tiryns and Mycenae seem thrown up by giants; Agamemnon's beehive tomb stands intact, a cavern out of the bright sun, to this day. It's hard to avoid the busloads of tourists there, the endless polyglot explanations; we hung about in the sun on this low fortified foothill until they'd all gone for lunch. And finally, the quiet of the early afternoon broken only by goat bells, we looked down the valley as Clytemnaestra must have looked, seeing her lord – his armies behind him, his mad captive Cassandra at his side – returning alive from Troy to his murder at home.

Before Schliemann dug up Troy, the scholars had it all worked out: the Trojan war was a solar myth. Now it is supposed to have been a trade war for control of the Dardanelles, not Menelaus' enraged recovery of his stolen Helen. My father told me of a story by Leo Amery in which the author meets an old man on a boat, and becomes more and more convinced that he is the still wandering Odysseus. He offers the old man this explanation of the war; and the old man nods, and says: 'Yes – yes; I daresay there's a lot in what you say; but then, you know – you never saw Helen.' A myth is not so easily destroyed.

In the Trojan war of Homer, in all the plays, the gods were part of the scene; not a decision, not a battle but the gods were in there, interfering. My father described the attitudes of the three major playwrights: 'Aeschylus said "This is what the gods do and isn't it splendid and right"; Sophocles just said "This is what the gods do"; and Euripides said "This is what the gods do and what a shady lot they are." They certainly seem so to us and indeed their private lives are so staggeringly immoral that I was at pains to discover just how far the Greeks really believed in them. 'I can't imagine that Socrates really believed in this comic set of crooks,' said my father, 'but of course their whole attitude to religion was quite different from ours. I always think of a statue of a boy praying, smiling up at the sky with his arms outstretched – not like Christians or Muhammedans with their posteriors in the air' (for the record, though, my father *did* also say that 'if you're going to have a religion – and I think you'll be very unhappy if you don't – Christianity is the least absurd').

To the Greeks, then, the gods were capricious and powerful; but they could take them with a bit of irreverence – indeed, in Aristophanes' *The Frogs* the booby of the whole play is the god Dionysus. And there's a perfectly easy explanation for the *number* of, say, Zeus' seductions: if each village has its legend about the father of the gods making love to a mortal – in one village in the form of a swan, in another as a bull – and then they all got joined up in a national religion Zeus obviously would plainly seem to have been indecently busy.

The rites of any particular god they might certainly take very seriously – particularly those of Apollo and the oracle of Delphi. There in a rocky cleft fell the sacred spring; there sat the priestess on her tripod, chewing laurel leaves and breathing the fumes that came up from the earth; as the guide engagingly put it, 'She fell in rupture by the exhaltations' and the priests interpreted what she said. 'They say the priests must have had a spy network all over Greece,' said my father, 'but there's not the slightest evidence for it'. With the steep thunderous cliffs behind, the rocks falling away to the valley where the god not once but twice sent a landslide to destroy an invading army, it was easy to believe that there'd certainly been something there – once. But an earthquake has blocked off the fumes; and even as early as the fourth century AD when a Roman Emperor who wanted to go back to the old gods sent to the oracle, he got only its last message: 'It's all finished here, and even the chattering spring has ceased to flow.'

And Delphi, in the end, did for city states, by letting in the one enemy they couldn't counter – Philip of Macedon, arch-intriguer; the conqueror from the north who only ever fought one battle, but said you could take any city in the world if you could get into it one donkey and a bag of gold. 'He managed to get himself included on the council that ran Delphi and from there he could intrigue away like blazes. Patriot orators like Demosthenes (he was the one who got rid of his stammer by orating at the waves with pebbles in his mouth) tried to warn the states. But they all said "Oh no, he doesn't mean any harm" – just like Hitler; at last Demosthenes did get them to face him in battle, but by then it was too late.

'People will talk as if what did happen must have been what ought to happen,' said my father sadly. 'They say "The day of the city states was over" – but need it have been? After a time someone assassinated Philip – a very reasonable thing to do – and then they all thought they could go back to their house matches; but they'd reckoned without his son' – and the son was Alexander the Great. True, he died when he was 33 but the damage was done: his generals carved up his empire into kingdoms, and that lasted until the whole lot was swallowed up by Rome.

Approach the classics and you find yourself peeling off Rome to come to Greece, beneath Greece discovering Athens; for my father the heart of the onion is Socrates the philosopher. He was an extraordinary man. Unlike most of the other philosophers, he didn't run a school: he was a stonemason who just pottered about the streets making fools of everyone who argued with him. We know about him from various writers, but mainly from Plato, and no one knows quite how much of Plato's 'Socratic Dialogues' were really what Socrates said. Between them they invented the theory of ideas (from which we get our word 'ideal'), the notion that this world is a sort of reflection of a greater one: our justice but a shadow of the ideal Justice, our truth a reflection of ideal Truth. And Plato also attributed to him his Republic, a truly ghastly utopia – whose basic notions are none the less attractive enough to be argued about still.

What obviously got my father, though, was less the philosophies than the man himself: this character who wouldn't take anything for granted, who questioned everything, who said 'Where the wind of the argument leads, there we *must follow*, without fear.' The attitude did for Socrates in the end, even in liberal Athens: he was had up on a charge of corrupting the young. The argument has a curiously contempory flavour: the young men weren't respecting authority any more, they were going round arguing with their betters and questioning everything they were told.

Probably all the prosecution had in mind was a spot of

banishment: but the form was that if a man was found guilty, the prosecution suggested a maximum penalty, the accused something lighter, and the jury chose between them. 'Death!' said the prosecution. 'Free meals in the town hall for the rest of my life!' suggested Socrates. This was plainly ridiculous, so the jury chose death – but even then everyone expected him to escape. 'No,' said Socrates, 'I've lived under Athens' laws all my life; I'll abide by them now.' And drank the hemlock they gave him, and died.

Greece was only the half of it, of course; but Rome owes to Greece an incredible amount. All the mythology: there were no stories to speak of attached to the Roman gods, so they simply applied the Greek ones to their own: the exploits of Zeus became Jupiter's, Venus took on the attributes of Aphrodite. Most of the philosophy: Lucretius developed Epicurean thought but he didn't invent it (and actually we've mostly got it all wrong – Epicurus believed in pleasure, all right, but he thought the only way to avoid disappointment was *not* to choose the pleasures of the flesh). And of course the writings: even in the time of Cicero educated Romans were just about bilingual, and Suetonius makes it clear that the last words of Julius Caesar were not, as Shakespeare has it, '*Et tu, Brute?*' but *και συ, τεκνον*? – 'you, too, my son?'

The Romans added roads; organisation; and a legal system which founded the laws of half Europe – though not, actually, our own. And they kept the peace of Europe – more or less – for longer than anyone else has before or since. But if you slice a real classic you're more likely to find 'Athens' engraved on his heart than 'Rome'. In the heyday of the classics St Paul's had one sixth-form master for Latin, one for Greek; the idea never caught on because too few would have chosen the Latin.

The old style of classical education is on its way out now, of course: the ancient world lies a second time in ruins. People learn classics, but not as they did under Hillard and Botting, one week Latin, one week Greek. It is supposed to be so narrow – but in some ways it was more modern than what has taken its place, with its set periods of 40 minutes and the GCE. It was a total immersion: in two cultures, two histories, two languages, two ways of thought: they learnt to write in Greek as well as just to read it. And any good master could bring in anything he thought the boys ought to consider: my father's boys knew about Milton and A. E. Housman and Hardy – and Bertie Wooster and Winnie-the-Pooh too, for the matter of that.

And to these classics, the culture-of-the-ancient-world short courses are no sort of substitute; for the linguistic training was crucial. 'If you get deep into another language you have to compare its thought with your own,' says my father. 'If you do a bad translation the chances are you haven't understood the English for a start. And you can't *waffle* in Latin,' he said, with a scornful snort at the whole smoke screen of Germano-American guff, against which the classic clarity shines, all bright and glittering in the smokeless air.

There were only two things wrong with a classical education. It took all the time there was, so you never learnt anything else – and this in the end was what did for it, of course. And there was a subtler disadvantage. Dealing with dead languages, problems that had long been solved, sums under which the line had finally been drawn, may have given the classically educated a feeling that it *had* all been done before, that there were no new answers; they may have wept like Alexander that there were no new worlds to conquer – but Alexander knew nothing of Russia and America and Australia.

Still, the classics could give a man a perspective and yardstick for his own times that a lot of us might envy. I feel inclined to say of my father what was said of another classic: 'His knowledge was not world wide; it was world deep.' And of how many other educations can you say more?

The Great Trek

Anyone want a purple lipstick? Four empty cassette holders? A file with its back broken from the strain of pretending that three readers' letters, a handout on Incontinence, and Sir Frederick Catherwood's lecture on the Diseconomies of Scale come in the same category? No? A pity; you could have had them for the asking last week. For we were moving office.

We were not off to Sheffield, the clean city with the low-class night-life or whatever its posters call it; just to another part of this complex of buildings. But short of actually soaking our breeches in tobacco juice to keep out the leeches, we could hardly have been more upheaved if we'd been heading up the Zambesi.

It did not bring out the best in us, though it brought out everything else. Some clung like dung-beetles on to their every last cardboard box, their cracked ashtrays, the Joke that had been on the wall since the last move: 'I'm very worried about that chair,' one secretary said. 'They say it's a health hazard with all that stuffing coming out of it, but J. L. Garvin sat there!' Others started throwing everything out with a sort of shipwrecked abandon, even taking their name-tags *off* any chairs or typewriters they didn't want to see again (though some of these did come round sufficiently to start rummaging through other people's dustbins later on).

Worst hit was the book section, always a-groan with volumes; when word got round that they were getting rid of six years' accumulated throw-outs, the hordes descended and cleaned out the shelves in an hour: 'It was like locusts,' said the assistant shakily. I didn't have the heart to tell her what was waiting for her at the other end: an immense crate of old copies of the *Financial Times*, the top one headlined 'Tapes will Clear Nixon.'

How it got there is not known; maybe the movers, who sweated away all through the weekend, thought we ought to be shaken up a bit; maybe the man who actually moved that crate was not one of the privileged three with a copy of the final plan. The one who moved us certainly didn't have one; and all those weeks of scheming to get our backs to our enemies, our desks placed so that we couldn't possibly provide a Good Excuse on X's route from his desk to his girlfriend, the relentless power struggle to get next to the kettle-plug – all went for nothing.

It was amazing what came to light – quite apart from the Top Secret box of D notices lost years ago, to which nobody can now find the key. The only girl who was not shamed by it all was the one who maintains a spotless office desk, and a spotless home, by dint of carrying all the mess in a briefcase ceaselessly back and forth on the Tube.

Folding umbrellas like dead spiders, plenty; all the tops of all the felt pens that have ever dried shacking up together in a hairy little Fuehrerbunker of their own, files so old that the words Immediate Action can hardly be discerned – all this one expects.

But who is this Agustin B. de Jesus on whose card I wrote Frozen Shrimps? And what about all those curious pieces of wire? Any page which mentions Good Buys gets sent a lot of fairly Bad Buys and they are sent back eventually, leaving only (it seems) a rack behind. There is now a thing called Industrial Archaeology, which mostly means rusting tin mines with foetid water at the bottom and John Betjeman at the top; I reckon we could now make a start on Office Archaeology, with carbon dating of letters: wouldn't even need to select choice things for future historians in a self-conscious box, just seal up any single desk and bury it.

We are getting straight by degrees. The Art and the Photographic are still pinching each other's bookcases, but that's OK – it's all the exercise they get; the telephones are alive again even if the telephonists don't seem to be. All the old files called Current Work have been turned the other way round and marked Archives; we have got over the shock of a drinking fountain in the ladies that looks exactly like a male urinal; and we are coming to enjoy the amenity of the new conference room which, being topped with glass, enables those not conferring to peer into it with the same sort of intrigued pity you feel at the Zoo.

But it's really something of a miracle the paper's come out at all this week. And if in fact it hasn't, and you aren't reading this, you will now at least understand why.

Don't tell me the Old, Old Story

There is something very odd about what happens to the old hereabouts. On the one hand, we give them too little pension, we bundle them off into awful wards and dreary Homes and there aren't even enough of those; we don't let them live with the young family as they do in Italy or boss the whole clan as in ancient China. On the other hand, there's a tremendous breast-beating about all this. Posters say 'punishing the old – a British way of life'; short spurts of boy scouts and task forces rush round painting their walls and defurring their kettles; we are all agreed that it's monstrous and terrible – and it goes right on happening.

With such a wide gap between what we do and what the people we pay to be our conscience say, there has to be a missing piece in the jigsaw. And I believe it's our squeamish refusal ever to say what we all know perfectly well: that a great many of the old are repulsive.

It isn't a question of blame; it's a question of fact. They may bump into you in shops because they don't see too well, but bump they do. Eating's tricky when your teeth won't stick but it doesn't make it any nicer to watch. They've plenty to grumble about, but a constant moan is a bore. Maybe they do like a nice sleep in the day because they can't sleep at nights – but getting the council to stop the boys ball-playing is a rotten thing to do.

And I wonder if we are right to assume that all this is something that can't be helped, or whether we simply aren't asking enough of them.

Because an awful lot of the old aren't like that in the least.

The last time I found myself sitting over a coffee in a motorway caf at 1.30 in the morning I was talking over the problems of schools with a 71-year-old who's a governor of both Roedean and Gordonstoun; she was pleased to be driven home since usually she'll drive herself the odd 100 miles or so. In the Philippines I stayed in a house that contained one woman who was off every morning at 6 a.m. to run a crèche in the University, and another who was sitting up in bed recovering from cancer with modishly painted nails signing cheques for the University of which she was president. They were both over 80. My father at 77 is into Meals on Wheels – not eating, delivering.

Eastern Airlines recently booted out the last of a long line of whizz-kids and reinstalled their antique founder; Casals and Picasso weren't noticeably geriatric before they snuffed it at 91 and 96; what about Matisse, what about old Golda, then? No one put her in a wheelchair when she turned 75. And one example that hit me between the eyes recently, reading about the Siege of Malta, was de la Valette, who throughout the whole of a sizzling summer held off the Turks by sheer force of will: making his knights slog it out day after tortured day, keeping even women and small children mending walls and loading cannon for as long as their wounds let them walk. This indestructible character was 74.

As soon as you list distinguished old people, of course, someone says 'Yes but you can't turn Joe Bloggs into Picasso.' No: but can't he go on being Joe Bloggs? I believe half the reason he doesn't is our deadly kindness in expecting him to take it easy, slacken off, stop trying; we turn him into a bit of old driftwood in the chimney corner – and then dislike him.

There was a recent *Guardian* article by a woman who had always scorned those who didn't have their old folks living with them – until her own moved in. The old pair treated the children like servants, switched off their son's TV programmes, left their teeth on the mantelpiece; from being a place where her children's friends automatically congregated, her home became somewhere they could hardly wait to leave. But why didn't she tell them *not* to leave their teeth on the mantelpiece, insist on fair shares with the TV? She was caught in a desperate contradiction between obligation and disgust, too nice to do anything about what was making her hate them.

And take this question of old people repeating things: they don't start doing it with a bang on their seventieth birthday – it starts gradually. Isn't it better to say 'you told me that already' than let them tell you a story ten times in a week – and then dread the next time you see them?

To ask anyone to be on the receiving end of other people's goodwill for twenty years or more is an inhuman demand – even if the goodwill holds out. And we might realise this better if we weren't so dishonest about how our normal social relations work. They are *all* get-something, give-something; some people amuse, some make others feel amusing; some make mince pies, some make money, some make a good shoulder to cry on. If we could admit that Aunty Maud is the biggest bore in Berkshire but a willing washer-up, we wouldn't say 'We can't ask the poor old duck to stand at the sink' – and then not ask her to anything. I put this view to an OAP on a phone-in once: 'Do you want us to work till we drop?' he asked piteously. If I'd had any guts I'd have said yes – the ones who do are the lucky ones.

The trend in modern geriatrics is to try to keep the old self-sufficient as long as possible: day care centres to keep them out of hospital, far more to do once they get in; the suggestion that the earnings rule be dropped is the first – no, second – sensible thing this Government's done. Even things like incontinence may be negotiable: put a doubtful case near a lavatory and hope for the best and he may hold out a lot better than one dumped in a distant bed with a pessimistic pad.

There's no earthly point in inventing drugs and operations

that keep the old young if we treat them all as has-beens the moment they're over 60. Brains, muscles, faculties atrophy faster if they don't get used. We should remember there's as big a gap from 60 to 85 as there is between 15 and 40. One 76-year-old said of another, 'she's let herself get so *old*'; she regarded it as a matter of the will, and maybe for more people it could be – if we didn't label them poor old granny and stuff them behind the curtains. And maybe we'd get a better deal for those who do need care, if we stopped pretending it was a matter of stroking silvery hair and picking up dropped handkerchiefs, and said it was coping with people who can be tiresome and unlovely and dull. Which sounds heartless and hard. But we've said all the soft things before; and it didn't get us far.

Never-Never Land

My brother cuts the time it takes to read a newspaper by skipping everything in the future tense; and it's amazing what he doesn't miss. Though it shouldn't be so suprising, when you think how guesses about the future get made. Some stick a pin in their horoscope (including at least one general in the last war). Some, with a computer to work out what isn't going to happen to at least fifteen decimal places, simply project all their existing graphs clean off the edge of the paper.

I have this vision that somewhere in the universe is the land of the Ex-Future, where Maplin shimmers in the distance, reached by the grid of monorails that was once to cover Britain. There, and only there, is that super-market we read about every five years, where the housewife of tomorrow will make a push-button selection of goods that will then be whizzed electronically down a tube into her basket (the latest super-market in Hampstead hasn't even got a car park).

In this never-never land, the people (all PhDs on account of equality) live in the House of the Future, designed over and over again by groups of Germans and Danes since the thirties. It is circular, has all the furniture in the middle of the room and a central plastic sink-bed-lavatory-desk-oven unit. Only it never got built because you'd have to send the whole thing back to the factory every time you needed to change a washer.

With such machines, it's always the human factor that breaks down: nobody votes the funds, or the country that was going to make it gets taken over. Or people's habits just don't build up in the expected way.

You might think, when the telephone's never been better, that people would rush across *less* to New York and Japan to clinch business deals. Or that, now that the Foreign Office can confer with any ambassador in a diplomatic whisper over the wire, Heads of State might not need to pop across to other countries. On the contrary. I have a vivid memory of all the droning delegates at a UNESCO cultural conference reading one another papers about how travel would become unnecessary because TV telephones would make five-continent conferences a commonplace; and there was *always* at least one of them not even able to get the right language on his simultaneous-translation headset.

People are always pointing out how the fantasies of Jules Verne and H. G. Wells came true in the end; but they were writing fiction. It's the people who think they're on to fact that provide the better laughs.

There was the careful Haldane calculation in the thirties that by now the population would have dropped so disastrously that there'd be nothing left but a few exhausted striplings busy pushing round the bath chairs of all the rest. And he was real, even if you couldn't say the same of the professor who in 1896 projected that if traffic increased at its present rate, by 1970 the surface of the globe would be covered six feet deep in horse manure.

Then there was the Austin Seven of the air, the certainty that by the 1960s we'd all be popping around in our little planes just as if they were cars. Before the First World War the future in the air lay plainly with huge dirigible balloons. And just before the Second World War, advanced opinion was all for sea-planes, since it would obviously be impossible to build runways big enough to take land-landings of sufficient length: it's a marvellous splash they make, in the land of the ex-future, taking off one a minute like Heathrow.

And as for things military, I forget what weapon it was that was first supposed to have made war so horrible that it could never happen again – the blunderbuss, probably.

One's personal ex-future, of course, simply doesn't bear thinking about – all those sentences beginning 'When I marry my millionaire . . . ' or one's certainty that one's own house would run like clockwork (no, correction – mine actually does: sometimes it goes slow, sometimes it goes fast, often it stops altogether – just like clockwork).

And remember how one's children were going to be brought up to be obedient *but* inquiring, to think for themselves *but* embrace all one's most treasured beliefs, to eat proper food – 'I got them into sensible eating habits from the start,' said Liz in a book by Celia Fremlin: 'just as if,' her friend commented, 'we had deliberately inculcated this craving for sweets and iced lollies against which we feebly struggled.'

No, it's more cheering to look at the Victorians, convinced that the London Missionary Society would shortly convert a thousand million heathen to Christianity; or Shaw saying that all sophisticated nations would shortly be following America's enlightened lead into Prohibition; or the countless revolutionaries who thought that that wicked capitalist frame-up, the family, would simply wither away under Communism, instead of being about the only thing in iron curtain countries that makes life bearable.

And does anyone recall Parity of Esteem, which was going to make it immaterial whether you went to a grammar, secondary modern or technical school – come to that, did anyone ever see a technical school? And this marvellous postwar certainty that there were going to be no more ugly buildings ever again, because democratically elected planning committees of shop stewards, lorry drivers, and tobacconists were going to have a look at all the plans first?

Things out of perfection sail, as Yeats said; and that's very often the last you hear of them.

Quack Quack

On the analogy of 'I am firm – you are obstinate – he is a pig-headed fool' most of us know that 'I am dying – you have flu – she has a slight head cold'. One of the hardest things to bear about any illness is other people's ideas about it: why can't they keep their filthy minds off our ailments?

Particularly, of course, when the minds are stuffed with antique notions of medicine. People with gout, suffering horribly with their smaller joints, are made worse by their rotten friends thinking (quite wrongly) that they got it by drinking port. Rheumatism equates with old age, in the popular mind ('on the private' they at least have the tact to call it fibrositis) though you get it before 40 as like as not. And a friend of mine recently came down with shingles, a vile disease caused by a virus akin to chickenpox – at least you can catch it from chicken-poxed children. It lodges in a nerve junction, sends false messages to the brain saying 'I'm burning!' and the brain obligingly orders up blisters. Worse than the actual agony, he said, was his friends' assumption that, since nerves were involved, he'd dreamed it all on himself – 'my nerves' being a Victorian lady's euphemism for any mental disorder.

It's extraordinary how outdated notions cling. People who've had TB, leprosy or a slight attack of goofiness have the greatest difficulty persuading anyone that these things are not both incurable and catching. You don't get sympathy if you've got anything considered low-class, like pink eye or rickets – much best describe it as contagious conjunctivitis and say you got your osteomalacia by sitting in a cellar hating milk. And modern terms aren't always better: men, for example, should never have been allowed near the concepts of premenstrual tension and menopausal gloom, since they now attribute to them any rages and tears whatever, even if they were caused by a perfectly just grievance.

Generally speaking, the less anyone goes near a doctor, the more they think they know about what's wrong with you – or themselves, for the matter of that. The woman who says 'It's lumbago and you know doctors can't do anything about that' plainly hasn't realised that a heart condition can make your arms ache, that a back pain can be anything from a slipped disc to a kidney to the onset of labour pains and that there seems to be almost nowhere in your body (as with the body politic) that can't be made ill by trouble somewhere else.

Nor do they appreciate that where it hurts and how green you feel is only a tiny part of the evidence – what about blood structure, pulse rate, temperature patterns and all the other things doctors spend years finding out about? And when they ghoulishly compare your bronchitis to Cousin Ethel's, they plainly don't realise the word is only geographical, tells you which bit of tube is in trouble – as if a plumber should say knowingly, 'It's pipeitis' for the knocking behind the radiator. Quite apart, of course, from the question of how badly you've got it. The high-water mark of artless idiocy in this field came from a child who gave her father mumps, which in turn gave him a ball the size of a grapefruit for several weeks. 'Your poor Daddy's been very ill,' said a sympathetic neighbour. 'Oh, no,' piped the babe, 'he had it the same as me only he made more fuss.'

The trouble is that you don't actually want people to ignore your illnesses; you just want to make sure they can't withhold sympathy by persuading themselves it's all your own fault anyway – if only because you haven't taken their tom-fool advice. The only way out, I think, is to take refuge in the decent obscurity of a learned language, like the P. G. Wodehouse cat

Augustus, who managed to get classed as *Traumatic Symplegia* what in anyone else would have been bone-idleness (he slept twenty-three hours a day). And if you don't know any medical terms, follow the clue provided by a man who said the other day that his wife was staying with an old lady 'hearing about her rare plants and her cystitis – for all I know cystitis is a plant'.

Precisely. Any flower catalogue will do – though I suppose you'd risk getting whisked off for an abortion if you said you'd got *lilium rubellum*. Next time I'm ill I'll say firmly that it's *hamamelis vernalis*, and wait for them to lay soothing witchhazel on my brow.

That, at least, ought to see me through till the doctor gets there with a euphemistic death certificate – like the one issued to Christian Buchan, who for thirty-five years had been a Burgess of Banff, was the Head of a Navigation School and died, an honoured grandmother, in 1893 of hepatic cirrhosis and myocardial degeneration. 'What's that?' asked her great-grandson wonderingly.

His doctor told him. 'The bottle,' he said.

Terribly Modern Manners

I was once told by a married friend that she'd fallen for another woman. So had her husband. The same other woman; and it was all mutual; and there they cosily were in a *ménage à trois*. You'd have thought that was problem enough, but while I was still trying to work out the basics, like who slept in which bed, she was on about the status problems: Is the wife in such a set-up dominant, the girl almost an au pair? Or conversly, the wife reduced to drudge Martha while Mary does nothing tougher than washing the master's feet?

Even on the wilder shores of love, apparently, there are problems about how to behave – good behaviour presumably being what it always was, which is not hurting people by accident. Yet there aren't any charts or navigation aids for these seas – let alone for the vast foreshore where it all overlaps with ordinary life. People living outside the conventions aren't known for being more forgiving or less touchy than anyone else; what we need is a manual on incorrect behaviour.

Many fathers who are resigned to their daughter sleeping with that young man, still don't know what to call him. Not fiancé or husband because he isn't; 'young man' sounds out of date and lower class, 'boy friend' sounds out of date and coy; and nothing is worse than aping the young in a boomingly horsy voice with 'and this is my daughter's – ah – fellow'.

When a son brings his girl down for the weekend, what's a fond mother to do about the bedding arrangements? Take his word for it that one bed will be fine? Or realise that a girl may well prefer to have a room in which to sulk and apply face cream; presumably one or the other of them will be able to make it across the corridor if they're sober enough for it to be any use.

How, if it comes to that, do you introduce any pair of what the social workers so charmingly call a Stable Illicit Relationship? You can really offend them by saying Mr and Mrs, and yet it's misleading to indicate nothing; I've only ever got out of it by saying 'This is Tom Smith – and Maggie.' The young, of course, have given up surnames, which ought to make things easier but doesn't: one got furious with his girl's father for saying 'I'm sorry there's no Mr Robinson here' when he'd been staying there for three months – but no one had ever called him anything but Bert.

As soon as you start on this sort of tack, of course, someone says, 'But why do you need to categorise people like this? Why can't you just accept them as they are without labels?' – though the last person who said this admitted that after forty minutes' conversation with a shaved monk in an aeroplane she simply *had* to know whether it was a man or a woman. But you need some sort of start: when you're trying to communicate you're surely picking up all the clues you can get. How old? – therefore what prejudices held or pushed aside? What country? – a remark about Vietnam from an American is not the same as from a Scot. What job? – or lack of it, or rejection of jobs? One isn't going to get far before some sort of guidelines are established.

The more mentionable things become, the greater the chance of saying the wrong thing. Take the unmarried mother. Few people nowadays would think of leaving her severely alone – but do you turn up at the maternity ward with a pair of pink bootees or not? I'd say not, because the worst brick you can drop is making the wrong assumption about what's to happen next: making her feel guilty about having it adopted by assuming she'll keep her baby, or weepy by assuming she's keeping it if she's not. Better stick to flowers and cologne.

Come to that, what about the white mother with a coloured infant? You assume it's adopted and you get a mortally offended proud mother; if you assume that the lady's had a sultry lover you may have put your foot in it again.

The manual, if it ever got written, would tell me when to start treating a pair of homosexuals as a married couple for inviting purposes; the difficulty is to work out how permanent the situation is. For all you know, your friend may be aching for an evening off from his ever-loving companion. Or worse, *he* may be happy to be asked out on his own, but the one left at home may be pining.

The two things homosexuals mostly loathe, incidentally, are constant joky references to their state to relieve the speaker's embarrassment; and being asked to perform as an Eligible Bachelor at dances. It's a mistake, too – and one which the enlightened are most likely to make – to assume that just because you know he's a homosexual, and he knows you know, then the matter can be openly referred to in company.

One of the hardest things to sort your way through tactfully is a messy divorce. You don't mention the ex unless your friend mentions him/her first, lest it cast a cloud; you don't say anything nasty in front of the children and it's apparently salt in the wound to say 'I always thought he was a swine anyway.' The paradox of our muddled view on it all is that although, on the one hand, we're so determined people should be free to follow their real feelings that we approve of their leaving home, we expect, on the other, that the remaining one should on no account show *her* real feelings by saying he's a louse to go.

There's a wealth of delicacy in a remark I heard Anne Scott-James make once, about being sure to invite X and Y before they got married, lest they think she was only nice to them once they were legal: still, they've broken up too now, so what the hell. Second weddings present plenty of problems to the innocent bystander – do you, or don't you, turn up with silver teaspoons and a hat as at a first wedding? Answer seems to be yes, if they invite you to any sort of binge – though you might check whether in fact they both got custody of the teaspoons in the courts.

The difficulty of having a manual for all this, of course, is that you'd need so many different people to write it – almost no one is under 20, over 50, divorced, Lesbian, father of an illegitimate baby and mother of a drug addict in prison. But the difficulty isn't going to go away – and for the same reason: nobody's an outsider in every way. The unmarried mothers maybe don't know how to talk to alcoholics, the homosexuals can be Indignant Ratepayers, the newly divorced can be furious fathers about the drug-taking young. Tolerance is splendid, but it doesn't get you everywhere. It doesn't mean you can put your foot in it, as the actress said to the – no, I mustn't make unkind cracks about the Church.

The Long Arm of the Lawyer

Counsel for the defence is allowed to object to up to six jurors for any reason or none. As the eighteen of us sat in the discreet modern court-room waiting to be called, the objections started. To women! I thought, blood beginning to boil. But no, they let through two, both young and pretty. Then older women, so –? They passed me. 'It's all right,' whispered a barrister, 'she's carrying *New Society*.'

Presumably the point is that when a young woman's accused, the chaps could feel a soft spot, the young things identify; only the cold fish eye of the woman of a certain age might stay undimmed by tears. Seems a questionable procedure, though, simply because if you're black or old or called McTavish (or, of course, carrying *New Society*) they know about it; if what you're suffering from is ulcers or fascism or a PhD, it doesn't show.

In the United States they're allowed to object to far more jurors and know a lot more about them; it's an accepted part of a lawyer's skill to boil down a jury in his client's interest. This is doubtless even worse: I'd have thought the sample should be as random as possible.

We were pretty random, even so: we included civil servants and an engineer, a train driver and two social workers, a milkman and a businessman. I cannot, however, speak for them – jurors are forbidden to say what goes on in the jury room, no doubt on pain of being blund on ye grunions and crayled on ye grotts.

The case was a complicated one of receiving stolen goods; the man had pleaded guilty on two of the many indictments;

his wife and a further dealer were charged with him. I was conscious all the time of a desire not to take the police word for it too easily – but at the same time of Sir Robert Mark's complaint that what makes the cops polish up the evidence is catching criminals, and then seeing them acquitted on a technicality.

It seems to me Sir Robert could turn his attention to the quality of the prosecution, among other things. Not being a lawyer I don't know if what I saw was typical, but there seemed an awful lot of pettifogging around, trying to prove little points that didn't matter at the expense of larger ones that did. No doubt the lawyers had their reasons, and who am I to say that being paid by the day was one of them. But I know I felt by the end of the first week that if I had to give a verdict then and there, it would be that cops might cook it a bit but were basically OK; crooks might crook it a bit but might well be OK; but as for the lawyers, they should be sent down for ten years each.

Of course, I realise that, to try to shake the prosecution case, witnesses must be disbelieved and overborne. But if a lawyer does this to some poor little guy who, whatever the rights and wrongs of this case, had undoubtedly been hit in the eyes with an iron bar during a jewel robbery, then you'd think he could at least show a decent restraint. Not at all: the three of them were like big cats licking cream when a good point was deemed to have been made. Three out of the four of them constantly said (as it were): 'Smiths' for 'Smith' – yet this was the sort of point they picked up like a flash in witnesses.

When the main defence lawyer was summing up I scribbled 'Ten more minutes of this and I'll burst into tears and go into receiving myself'. It's some small consolation that it was the man with the most eloquent lawyer who copped the sentence, so at least these creatures don't decide everything.

The days wore on: hallmarks and identification of rings, of

coins, of this bit of loot, of that. There were moments when it was hard to believe that police, judge, lawyers and all witnesses were not in as great a muddle as I was; see what a tangled web we weave when first we practise to receive.

All the time I was longing to see beyond and behind the evidence, to ask more: there was so much the social worker could have found out, that a journalist could have found out, if it had been permitted. I know it's supposed to be a great strength of our system that the jury has to assess only the facts, to ask has it been proved or hasn't it? But the trouble is that when you're trying to work out who to believe you need to know what is probable, what that world is like: is that how things are done in pubs? in Cutler Street Market? do people often buy watches on the pavement outside the Wimpy Bar in Stamford Hill?

I found myself wishing that instead of this cops v. robbers war, one could have a more middle-of-the-road inquiry, such as an examining magistrate has the right to in France. True, the judge is allowed to ask questions; but the whole point of us, the jury, was the wide variety of experience, age, class, job, and so on, we offered; yet we were not allowed to ask such general questions at all.

So the final day came. One of the ushers was sworn on pain of something or other to lock us in and never speak to us again save to say 'have you considered your verdict?'– so it was the other who asked us if we'd like some sandwiches. We were out for five hours.

The man was found guilty, his wife and the secondary dealer not guilty; several of the verdicts were by majority, and I guess if this had been twenty years ago, before they had such things, the whole wretched business would have had to have been done again.

As we took our expenses and went away, there was none of the joyous feeling of being off the hook that we'd been looking forward to for a fortnight. 'I feel it's tainted money,' said one. And another swore 'Goddammit, now I feel *sorry* for him!' The young school teacher, whose half-term holiday had been swallowed up entirely, was quietly crying.

The sentences ran concurrently; to start with he'd pleaded guilty to enough to let him in for that amount. If there were no fences there would be no armed robberies. But sending a man to prison for three years is never a happy way to spend the day.

What Every Woman Knows

Anyone who lets a woman into business hopes she will surmount her natural disadvantages as best she may, showing no more weakness than is native to her sex. But is it not time, on the contrary, that the men picked up a few of the traditional idiocies of women?

Take the pension problem, for example. Firms fuss endlessly about how to retire Joe Soap, plainly past it at 58, keep on Steve Bean, whizz kid of 66, and not have everyone down the line feeling aggrieved and insecure because of it. The root of the trouble is that, however the two men look or behave, everyone *knows* that Steve is older than Joe. Wouldn't the problem be solved if they'd only keep their ages secret, the way women do?

Again, women are supposed to be a bad bet for high office because they have moods – at least that was what they were called before they were reclassified as pre-menstrual tension or menopausal disturbance, depending on how long they – moods and women – had been going. But at least women can, presumably, say straight out 'that was a bad decision; I made it on an off day'; men aren't so lucky. Anybody who lives with one knows that any man has immense changes of pace and temper too; yet since theirs aren't cyclic they're not predictable, like the tides; just devastating, like the weather.

But because there's no timetable reason why a man is sluggish one day, a fool the next and brilliant by turns, everyone has to pretend he is the same yesterday, today and forever more (though even St Paul had the sense to reserve that one for the Almighty). Wouldn't people like Wilson and Chaban-Delmas be only too grateful for a ready-made reason why they dropped this brick or that?

This misleading pretence of uniformity crops up again with clothes. At first sight, it's a great disadvantage for women to have to lug around suitcases with a change of dress while the briefcase brigade bound off the aeroplane with nothing but a couple of shirts and an alert expression. But you could put the thing the other way round and say what a pest it is that the chaps give so little away by their appearance.

A woman who went on wearing what was the OK garb for a gentlewoman of thirty years ago would be suspected of having ideas to match; if she turned up backless and frontless she'd be making the same sort of statement as a youth driving a red sports car with no silencer. But the men don't make any statements at all, since they all wear the same suit year in year out (I know designers and writers and human beings vary it a bit; not businessmen). One could allow a lot more accurately for their types and tastes, sexual pretensions, backgrounds and temperament if they didn't act as though they'd be court-martialled if found out of uniform – and without even the helpful pips and crowns of a distinguishing rank.

Again, it's said of women that they never manage to keep their minds on just one thing; that they're thinking of the price of tea even as they listen to the chairman's annual review. I'd say it was entirely arguable that the ability of men to shut the door of boardroom and Cabinet, and never let their minds stray to the thought of actual people buying tea, was the root of half our troubles.

The last thing we ought to want is conformity to the male pattern. On the contrary we ought to be able to bring some relief from the tribal tyrannies of men: from the need to reinforce their own image in the eyes of their mates, which has such marvellous parallels among the hide-hunting Bantu (quite beautifully shown in the Leyland strike, when practically all the men wanted to go back to work, but nobody dared to seem less resolute than the next he-man along). The pity of it is, of course, that it so seldom works out that way: too many newly arrived women feel obliged slavishly to copy what's there already, just to get accepted at all. And it's all the more ironical when there are plenty of more enlightened managements these days which are really feminine in style.

For what, when you come down to it, is all this stuff about participation and consultation and communication, but the belated realisation that the way people react to your ideas is as important as the ideas themselves: that people matter? The last time I was told women were no good in business I was having breakfast in a train with a pert salesman who kindly explained that management consisted of persuading people to do things; and it was well known that women were useless at that – so much for Aspasia and Lady Gregory, Lady Bessborough and Diane de Poitiers, not to mention Marcia Williams. It's now fashionable to say you can get results, or get the credit, but not both; I'd have thought women had known this all along.

Some years ago I was enraged, in a fight with a picture editor, to hear that he was saying 'Why is she so against me? She doesn't even know me!' when the matter was, as I saw it, an entirely abstract problem. How feminine these men can get, I thought disgustedly; but I now think I may have been wrong. If we could have worked out some compromise – met and agreed the pictures, shared some personal exchange – maybe things would have been better. I hope I would not now take so uncompromisingly masculine a line.

Term Time, Thank God

No, I'm sorry, I haven't time to write an article this week; what with taking back the new football boots because one of the boys had said he needed new ones, and then found out he'd been trying on the wrong pair; and when I got back from that, being told by the other that he'd just found out *he* needed boots, because he hadn't, oh, sorry, tried his on when I had asked him to try on everything two weeks ago. . . .

Still, at least the holidays are over. I daresay those who pushed their children off to boarding school ten days ago have begun to feel the balm of forgetfulness stealing over the raw wounds of the summer, but we day-school parents at least have a constant reminder of how lucky we now are to get a few hours a day to ourselves.

If you ask me, the main reason for the 1870 Education Act was that parents, prevented by philanthropic Acts from sending their children down the pits or up the chimneys any more, had to find some other way to get them out of the house.

It's not that I've anything against children, beyond the fact that they are demanding, noisy, given to sulks and tempers and staying in their pyjamas all morning and then saying, 'But you *said* we could go to the toyshop!' two minutes before lunch.

It's just that it's marvellous to be able to walk down the road without picking the Coke rings out of the gutter, to listen to the wireless without the inevitable cries of Gerrorf! or that tuneless whistling that seems to accompany all the educational ploys so warmly recommended on uplifting women's pages. It's nice to be able to read a letter without finding six reasons why I don't have to play Monopoly or go swimming; sheer shrieking boredom and the fact that it's pouring with rain not being accepted as an excuse in either case.

Forgive me if I sound jaundiced. But this is the time of year when those professionally concerned with children come back bursting with interest and good intentions and clichés about how they learn more from the children than the children do from them – which, if true, could be the nation's only good excuse for paying them a babyminder's salary.

The battered parent is less keen on this Neo-Wordsworthian conviction that our attempts to halfway civilise our children only spoil their pristine creativity, their clear-sighted, unsullied directness. The people who hold it see the children during those hours when they *are* eager and inquiring. They don't have to listen to their conversation at meal times.

'They bring a fresh approach,' which is why they think jokes like Adam and Eve and Pinch Me funny all over again, from generation unto generation; why they start from scratch on solving the world's problems, 'they ought to shut up all the bad men in prison before they do any robberies' or 'why don't they pull down all the ugly factories?' 'They're full of such spontaneous energy', which is why they can't sit in the back of the car for twenty minutes without fighting. Yes, yes, I know you can't expect them to, but that's what I'm complaining about. I just wish they'd go and trail their clouds of glory somewhere else.

These unsullied children of nature think Scooby-doo is funny, Coca Cola is a drink, their ankles would break if they had to walk half a mile, and that soap weakens the body (pure hearsay, this, it's not as if they used the stuff). And they are, of course, honest – which is why they will assure you with open-eyed candour that every other child in the class has five pounds a week pocket money and goes to bed at two in the morning. (We will not speak of their mothers, who say they all get twopence a month and have the light out by half-past five.)

When they finally go to bed, I sit and dream of my heroes: Harry Graham, who said 'It must be ages since I ceased / To wonder which I liked the least'; W. C. Fields: 'No one who hates children can be all bad'; Patrick Thornhill, who recommended to a sentimental committee which wanted to lay on a traditional celebration for the children, that they revive the practise of beating the boys around the parish boundary. And Mary Stott, who cheered us all by pointing out that A. S. Neill's 'There are no bad children, only bad parents' was as cruel in its way as the Victorian conviction that it was always the children who were wicked.

Indeed, I can't help wondering if we aren't even beastlier to our children than we need be just because we're so often told they are always the innocent party.

One final word of warning to those who are about to write and say that it's only the foul way I've brought up my own that gives me this degraded view of children. I may, indeed, have been harsh about my own. But just don't start me on other people's. Just don't *start* me.

Up the School

'My Lord Mayor, ladies, gentlemen, girls and boys – it gives me great pleasure to welcome you all here today to the prizegiving of St Cerebral's. I am particularly gratified to see so many of our distinguished board of governors on this platform; we know they are exceedingly busy men, so it is hardly surprising that many of us have not had the opportunity to meet them much, or indeed at all, during the past academic year. But I am sure pupils and teachers will join with me in expressing to them our deep gratitude for all that they do for the school.

'During the past year we have had our little difficulties, but we have had our successes, too. We had eight A-level passes in Mathematics, ten in English, to name but a few; and I think we can pride ourselves that, for a grammar school, we give a more broad-based education than many; this is shown by the exceptional number of CSE passes in Geography, Cooking, Woodcraft and Needlework – ninety-six in all won for the school. Many of our pupils are this term leaving us for further education; as Browning said: "A man's reach should exceed his grasp", or what's competition for? And I am glad to say that though many boys and girls tried for scholarships to Oxford and Cambridge, the majority have now decided to be loyal to the locality, a fact to rejoice the hearts of my colleagues at the Slowgrind Institute of Advanced Technology.

'Nor, in pursuit of *mens sana*, have we neglected *corpore sano*. It was perhaps unfortunate that the development scheme attached to the Uphill works estate has temporarily lost us the use of our playing field; however we have it from the best authority – the local authority (*laughter*) – that they expect the bulldozers to be gone by next spring or at very latest the following autumn. In the meantime, our teams have played some splendid "away" matches, putting up a very creditable show against St Crutch's (lost 5–6), the village team of Nether Millstone (lost 4–6) and scoring a thumping victory against St Hilda's (won 48–nil). I understand there was some confusion about this fixture, originally planned for the girls' Senior Hockey team; but we always forgive success where we find it, ha-ha, and I congratulate our boys on a really admirable result.

'It is always my pleasure on these occasions to thank the staff for their untiring efforts and great loyalty to the school, and I do so most heartily now. I am only sorry that out of the 102 teachers who have set the pearls of wisdom before you in the past year only six are able to be with us today; but I am encouraged to feel that with this splendid nucleus of "old hands", if I may so describe you, we shall have a very strong teaching team next term.

'Looking back on my forty-four years in the school, man and boy, I am constantly astonished to see how the picture has changed. The blazer, the gym tunics, the school hymns may be much as they were, the buildings stand immemorial; but elsewhere – what a transformation! When I was a boy, the most we aspired to was an outing up the River Mudde, and there were many parents, in those days, who could not even raise the necessary 3*s*. 6*d*. But now! – One school outing has been to Norway and another to Paris – imagine the joy of seeing with young eyes for the first time the Sacré Cœur – Notre Dame – the Boulevard St Germain – *ses étudiants, son église, ses pissoirs!* as the guide says; a treat enjoyed by every single member of the fifth and sixth forms who remembered to bring to school the necessary £38 10*s*.

'It is my pleasure to pay tribute to the many efforts of our Parents' Association. They have held, I believe, as many as nineteen coffee mornings, three jumble sales and a puppet show specially put on by Tom Glover's father, who is Glover of Glover's puppets; further interest in puppetry was also stimulated by Mr Glover's offer to sell at a discount a number of puppets in discontinued ranges. Through all this, they have raised £14 10*s*. towards the new gym equipment, and we now only await a substantial contribution by the local authority before buying it.

'If I have dwelt at length on our recent past achievements, it is not, I think I should say, because we are not a forward-looking school. We have accepted, for example, that the sixth form should not wear uniform, and mini-skirts are for the first time being seen in their classrooms – though I make no apology for banning the trailing maxi-coats which are hardly suitable for a mixed school.

'One of our boys submitted a sculpture – a very moving crucifixion quaintly entitled "Hangup" – to the local Art Schools competition, where it got an Honourable Mention; and we now have our own experimental cinema where we have shown such "advanced" films as *Rififi* and *Les Enfants du Paradis*. I know some boys were disappointed that we did not permit the showing of *Flesh*; I can only assure them that the decision was not taken lightly, but only after very careful perusal of the film by myself and most of the staff.

'In conclusion I can only say that we have in the past year kept up the traditions which have made St Cerebral's what it is, coupled with the truly modern outlook which we would all agree that we share.'

Keep Your Hair On

I believe in changing hairdressers for the same reason as changing bank managers, just to show I can; but it's a bit like changing a heavy suitcase to the other arm; it's never better for long.

Why, I thought wearily as I crawled out after nearly four hours last week, do they classify hairdressing as a service industry? Nothing could be further from the truth. Time was when I thought there were only two sorts of hairdressers, those who wouldn't do what you wanted and those who couldn't; now I wish I didn't know just how many variations there are.

There's the very grand place, where you have to tip about eight people even to get to the basin; it is stuffed with women I used to think went to the hairdresser's in their best clothes (how odd), until I realised they probably don't have any others: there's a world of difference between the way the rich dress to show what they can afford, and the way the rest of us dress, to conceal what we can't. These hairdressers may give you a very pleasant time, along with your inferiority complex, but they don't bother with what *you* think you want – why should they?

Then there's the up-and-coming place where you have to have the boss man because he's the only person around who can cut without the aid of a lawnmower; but, as he's also the proprietor, he's forever leaving you dripping while he rushes off to have little managerial dust-ups with his suppliers or to see to the installation of an infra-red cooker for the Health Food Bar.

Whatever they don't happen to have – beer for setting,

lacquer, a dry towel – they imply is out of fashion; and they employ tall, self-conscious young men in intensely tight trousers whose bursting fly is exactly at eye level, so you crick your neck trying simultaneously to keep your head over the basin and modestly avert your eyes.

And there's the same thing a few years later, when it's all going down; cobwebs behind the ferns, scuffs on the matt beige paint; dim chits languidly wash one side of your head only with their flaking mahogany talons and sniff as they bring you the health food, now degenerated into a pile of grated carrot and a gritty bit of bread that tastes like smokeless fuel.

So it's better out in the suburbs, where things are less smart, perhaps, but less hectic? The hell it is. Same endless waiting – they can *none* of them resist the temptation to over-book on a busy day; same sneers: 'Who on earth cut your hair last?' (the only possible answer is 'Vidal Sassoon, why did you ask?'); same mindless chat about the hot passions of their boy friends as they fail to notice that the tap is running cold. And, on a slack day, an air of somnolence so great that I seriously thought the last one I tried must be stationed over a leaking gas main.

It doesn't get any better wherever you go, it's just that the people in the pink overalls are fatter and fiercer. I found a place in Bourneville that still has you hanging your head forwards into the sink; and there's a lady in Wellington, New Zealand, who was still doing marcel waving from the first time round when it came back again.

Only in hotels and on ships do they do a brisk impersonal job, since they're plainly not going to redesign every one-night stop-over; and only with them do you get peace: I forget who it was who when asked 'How do you like your hair cut?' replied 'In perfect silence.'

Over the years I've evolved a few primitive survival techniques. I've learned a smattering of their language: I know that 'You need a conditioner' means 'We need the money'; that

'Oh it's not dry *yet*' means 'He's still two clients behind.' I realise by now that if you ask them to squeeze you in, you're asking for trouble, and that the only times of day when you just may get through fast are early morning (if they're up) and last thing when they're racing to be away.

I know that a cut that you can blow-dry yourself means you can at least be miserable in your own home, and I've learned to take a very long and boring piece of work with me and make no further appointments that day. I've found that alongside most flapdoodling Monsieur Alphonses there is a quiet overworked female who is less flamboyant, less apt to be away organising a fashion show and much less given to cutting off every hair you've got just to prove it's spring.

And I know that the reason the faces of old peasant women look so serene under their kerchiefs is not because they're close to nature or even because all their children have grown up. It is because they have never, in all their lives, been to the hairdresser at all.

The Open-Plan Family

The kibbutz may be changing out of all recognition in Israel. Yet the kibbutz ideal increases its grip on the world year by year. Communal groups, Women's Lib groups, any set of people keen to redesign the family, all look to the kibbutz as the one experiment in communal living that has really worked – worked not just because it plainly holds together and prospers, but because it does so without compulsion. And if the idea of the kibbutz were even to disappear in Israel while it took root all over the world, it wouldn't be the first time (witness Judaism and Christianity) that such a bird has flown from its Palestinian nest.

What the message of the kibbutz actually *is* is another matter. It's entirely possible that the message we get isn't the authentic transmission at all. One of the biggest ironies of the Middle East today is that every summer flocks of starry-eyed young people, chafing from the bonds of capitalism and family, yearning for a freer world, pour into what is in fact one of the most highly structured systems in the world. It comes as a shock to some of them to realise that fair shares for all means everyone having their prescribed tasks; their set hours (like, they even have to get up in the morning); their pocket money. Even trivial things like soap and toothpaste are either rationed (if they're any good) or are awful enough to make sure that nobody uses more than they absolutely have to. For the visiting idealist it's easier to pool money and property, than to accept that you can't even borrow the Land-Rover or take a week off without a committee decision; and they realise with wonder that the kibbutz-reared young, visited by the footloose of half the world, aren't themselves free to travel at all.

A similar myth invests their human relationships. There are dozens of standard kibbutz jokes about people turning up expecting a sexual free-for-all from which anonymously fathered children fall into the communal Moses basket; and finding instead a close network of fathers and mothers, grandmothers and grandfathers. 'It's the most family-angled place I've ever seen in my life,' complained one; and another, relating a sad tale of a woman who'd attempted suicide because her husband had an affair, commented, 'I don't see how anyone *manages* an affair in a kibbutz. It's like a village, everyone knows everything.' Of course, the younger kibbutzniks are more free, and there are divorces and occasional shifts around; but, if anything, less than elsewhere. When I went to Yad Mordechai I met a girl pushing a pram, at what seemed to be an odd hour for a mother to be with her baby; I learned that she was on her way out, as she had a disrupting effect on newcomers. 'She is too free,' they said disapprovingly.

But it is to the freedom from child-rearing that the women of the world look with the greatest longing – or the greatest misgiving. Over the years the Women's Lib aspect of the kibbutz has been much eroded. You tend to find the females most in the laundries and kitchens, in the baby-house or perhaps on the cultural committees; and though there are a few well-publicised women kibbutz presidents, and jobs are supposed to be rotated, the rotation, like a bent roulette wheel, is a little apt to stick when the right people are at the top. Arguments rage as to whether this reversion is due to chauvinist male piggery – 'When I first came they let me drive a tractor – not now,' one woman said wistfully; or whether it's the women themselves who have realised that heave-hoing in the open field is no great shakes except ideologically. Certainly it is often the women who are rebellious about kibbutz arrangements. 'I wanted to stay, but my wife didn't,' is a common explanation for leaving; or, as one girl put it, 'I spent three months ironing the bras; such *big* bras, too' – it seemed a symbol of lost liberation.

There has been a similar shift in the way children are brought up – though probably not for the same reasons. In the beginning the babies went into the baby-house a few days after birth, with the mothers visiting to breast-feed; everything within the children's house was rigidly controlled; germs, even on the moustaches of grandfathers, were rigorously excluded. The children only saw their parents for the statutory 4–7 after-work visit.

This was partly due to the ideology, of course, but it also fitted current doctrines of child care: whatever else rearing children in children's houses does, it leaves them nakedly exposed to the winds of child-care theory. Whereas the regimented rearing of the thirties was probably watered down in other countries by inefficiency and tradition and maternal impulse, in the kibbutz it was given to the last full-strength drop. And a good many people resented it.

'I hated saying goodnight to my mother at 7,' one woman recalled. 'I had a brother and I was always going down to see him and getting chucked out of the baby-house.' This woman, who left the kibbutz when she grew up and married an American, remembers trying to explain herself to the kibbutz committee: 'I felt they were all my parents' generation, they weren't understanding *me*.' Psychologists coping with the casualties of the system pointed to 'parental deprivation' – just as psychologists across the world in America were pointing to parental over-exposure.

But these rigours are a thing of the past – at Yasur, I wandered easily in and out of baby-houses with a grandfather off duty; it is no longer the *metapelet* or night watch who copes in the night, but the mother, connected by baby-alarm to her child.

I met a girl whose son had just had his hair cut: 'The psychologic woman says in his age it is important he know he is a boy,' she said – so much for Absolute Equality. In some of the kibbutzim the children even sleep at home – though in only 24 out of 224 so far: it's a vast work rejigging the actual buildings, where the dwellings were built for couples not families.

Some of the pressure for this has come from the kibbutz psychologists; but much has been wrested from the old ideologists by the young mothers who have grown up in kibbutzim. I met one girl, engaged to another kibbutznik, who said she'd never give *her* baby 'to be looked after by a stupid *metapelet*'; and this push from the young kibbutz girls towards a closer contact with their children is widely used as a condemnation of the system. It could, however, be seen as exactly the opposite – if you consider, yet again, the Harlowes and their monkeys. The Harlowes raised monkeys in varying degrees of deprivation – some had mothers but no playmates, or vice versa, some had plenty to eat but nothing to hug, and so on. The conclusions were two: first, that the ones with a peer group but no mother did better than any other group except the ones with both (much better than those with a mother but no peer group); and, second, that a female monkey that had been badly mothered showed it by being a lousy mother itself. If it is the girls who were raised by the kibbutz method who are demanding more chance to mother their babies this doesn't suggest – even though they endured the system when it was a great deal tougher than it now is – that *their* instincts were particularly damaged by the process.

The importance of the peer group, as opposed to the parents, has always been a central debating point about kibbutz education. Does the continuity of the group mean that children depend too much on those of their own age, are too reluctant to offend them, too conformist? Does the fact that the boys and girls live, eat and sleep together until they're 18 mean that they get so used to inhibiting sexual responses to these fake siblings that they're generally inhibited later on? The kibbutzniks and ex-kibbutzniks never stop arguing about it.

Certainly the boys and girls generally meet their mates in the Army – the bod in the next bed is not so alluring when you remember that it used to be in the next cot. But it's worth remembering that the parents are a good deal more around than, say, the parents of British children at boarding school; that during the three hours of the day when the children *are* at home, the parents are free to talk and play with them – a very different pattern from the day-long half-attention of the ordinary busy urban mother. And fresh light was indirectly thrown on the whole situation by the publication of Ure Bronfenbrenner's *Two Worlds of Childhood.*

In this book, he contrasts the child-rearing methods of the States and the USSR, with a few sideswipes at other countries (including ours) thrown in. The Russian method is to use the peer group to get across the ideology: carefully guided but feeling they're doing it all themselves, the children train one another. 'Ivan hasn't got good maths marks this week, Ivan is letting down his row; Natasha will go home with him every day next week and help him' – with the teacher stepping in when the class proposes, for example, too alarming a punishment for some infant malefactor. The 'classroom collective' is the dominant influence, though the children spend a lot of hours each day with their parents.

In America, by contrast, the peer group is *thought* to be less important – nobody (except chewing-gum manufacturers) consciously manipulates it, and the parents imagine they are bringing up their children themselves by direct communication. Bronfenbrenner shows, though, that in terms of actual hours spent, actual influences, actual formation of ideas, it's the peer group that counts in America, too – but a peer group that's entirely undirected. Parents, far more than they think, simply leave the children to their own devices: the kids are in the rumpus room, down the yard, away at camp, watching TV. This means, he thinks, that the ideas of the children tend to come out as a sort of lowest common denominator of what six-year-olds think, what ten-year-olds think and so on. Slotting the kibbutz into this scale, it seems a pretty fair compromise: *more* parental attention, and a peer group more wholesome than in America, but less angled than in Russia.

And in Israel, of course, the kibbutz-reared are regarded as extra well brought up, not the reverse: their performance in exams (even when the variables of their selection have been ironed out) is better than average; they produce an overly high proportion, not just of devoted cannon-fodder, but of pilots who need personal initiative; the arguments about how they have been taught to rely on themselves, not to run to Daddy, how they respect rules because they see the sense of them, how they make their own discipline reminded me irresistibly of public school apologists in Britain (though it naturally enraged anyone I suggested it to, the ideology being so different). 'It's so good for the boy that there is not this tension with his father,' one explained. 'When my son drove the kibbutz car into the river, and then got a tractor to fish it out, and drove *that* into the river, and then did the same with the *other* tractor, it was the kibbutz he had to go to, not me.' Another boy who thought the kibbutzim were too materialistic ('we *ought* to go back to having all the same shirts') said: 'I respect the council because it's not "they", it's "us".'

If half the gloomy predictions of some psychologists were true, the kibbutz-reared would be a set of low-key conformists unable to feel or act without the approval of the group; but the very flexibility which has led the kibbutzim into the age of industrialisation seems to suggest exactly the opposite. One young man said he thought the effects of the kibbutz on his fiancée were a good deal less than the effects of, say, an all-girls school, and another pointed out that it's only a social taboo that stops actual brothers and sisters leaping into each other's beds; no reason, he thought, why the taboo – in any case not complete – that keeps members of a group from finding each other too thrilling sexually should have any worse effect.

How much, though, can the kibbutz idea transplant? Even those who find the wine headiest often doubt if it will travel. Yehuda Paz, a young sociologist working in Jerusalem, thinks you need, first, a unit that has some natural reason to hold together, as the farm or factory unit holds the kibbutz: it would work, say, with a scientific research unit stuck out in the country. Again, it has to be geographically small – so much of what goes on, with the children especially, makes sense only because a child can walk to its parents' house, or a mother can pelt out in her pyjamas if the nightwatch rings the alarm, without having to cross a lorry route on the way. And naturally it has to be a unit with some sort of financial autonomy, to be genuinely communal at all.

But possibly even less transplantable is the feeling that the kibbutz-reared people are an *élite* (Dorothea Krook even wrote a long paper proving they were a landed aristocracy). It's not just that it may be psychologically important to be thought of as the golden children of your society, rather than a bunch of hayseed cranks; but that the central dilemma of *any* voluntary commune is that it's a better option for the duds than the doers: it's harder for the man who could perfectly well earn his own car and stereo, to wait patiently until the kibbutz can afford them for all (and not *all* kibbutzim are stinking rich). In the ordinary way the brighter sparks might simply go, leaving a collection of second-raters to struggle on as best they could. It is the ideology, the terrific respect the kibbutz enjoys in Israeli thinking, that keeps enough brilliant men in them to make the thing a success; and it's hard to think of another situation to parallel it. Of course, you can simply pass laws to force people to be communal – but that immediately infects the situation with the entire range of totalitarian diseases.

And even the child-rearing system might be different elsewhere. It, like any other educational system, is a filter between parent and child, so it depends on what's being filtered. In Israel the force to be filtered is the fierce protective love that through the centuries has made a Yiddisher momma go in rags rather than send a boy out to work before his schooling was finished. Given too much affluence, it can turn into Mrs Portnoy; diluted by kibbutz methods, it probably ends up at about what others would consider normal strength. The same system, with a colder family climate, might turn out very differently.

But for all that, two lessons from the kibbutz seem clear. Children could probably tolerate far more away-from-parent care, provided it was the right sort, than most in our society have: to use the occasional kibbutz bed-wetter and a set of vague fears about deprivation as a reason for holding back on nursery schools, for example, is moonshine. But equally, if the kibbutz system works, it does it with the family at its very centre.

The original idea may have been that, deprived of its economic stranglehold, the family would cease to exist: the kibbutz proves that it apparently needs no economic sanction at all. Somewhere, some day, they may invent a useful alternative to the family; this certainly isn't it.

The Ouch Account

It's a pity doctors can't prescribe a dose of their own magazines for their more depressed patients; for there's no quicker cheer-up than a whiffle through the medical advertisements. Advertisements, that is, in medical mags which the patient isn't supposed to see.

The cheer is twofold. It's comforting to think that no matter how bent and decrepit one may some day become, there's still an opening for the model prepared to swear she's a martyr to her varicose veins, doc, or imitate the racked action of an acid-stomach sufferer. The other half is the ads themselves.

There are the admen, do you see, using all their streamlined Madison Avenue techniques on unspeakable things like skin eruptions and infections of the upper colon; and my God if they had trouble not recommending a Japanese product with the phrase 'from those wonderful people who gave you Pearl Harbour', it's nothing to the headaches they face doing the happy, strong, sexy, reassuring bit on things mainly designed to make you go to hospital less or to the lavatory more.

Here, for example, we have the medical version of Somebody's Mother Isn't Using Persil Yet: a small boy saying 'My 'petigo went quicker than yours did . . . so there!' – this for some cream that Stops Impetigo In Its Tracks – and in yours, too, I daresay, if that's where you happen to have it.

A glossy head is not there to sell shampoo so much as a cure for seborrhoeic dermatitis; and the version of 'And-then-I-tried-Horlicks' is a mother forever getting the kids to school late and leaving the theatre early until she gets this miraculous diarrhoea-preventing gunge.

Mind you, I sympathise. How *do* you set about making an ad about urinary infection? 'Look, we tried photographing the germ, only it looked like Marlon Brando; we gave them a realistic old biddy last time, they said the GPs saw too many of them anyway – why don't we just do a nude, like the auto industry?' Which they did – a lovely bronze torso, only marred by the little white words across it saying 'a bacteriological study of over 23,000 urinary pathogens showed that . . .'

But it's a bit unnerving to think of a GP actually prescribing something because of a little rhyme saying 'Constipation Plagues the Nation; Most will give a Laxative; Instead of purging we are urging Think laterally—restore bowel rhythm naturally . . .' Actually all laxatives claim to work 'naturally' (what's the opposite, for Pete's sake?) just as all painkillers work quicker and all strong drugs are (it says here) less addictive. I suppose after a while the doctors get deadened to the advertising just as we do.

I will always treasure in my memory, though, the stuff described as The Delicious Way to Treat Threadworms. Yes, thank you, doctor, how kind of you to ask; the threadworms pushed off years ago and now I drink it with gin.

Green-Eyed Monster

Whatever else is wrong with you nowadays, it better hadn't be jealousy. Admit that you are layabout, frigid, manic, cross-eyed or convinced that you're a poached egg, and everyone will do what they can to sympathise. But if you're jealous – you're out.

The situation was well described – and deplored – by Karen Durbin in a remarkable article in *Time Out* some while ago – remarkable because *Time Out* is the magazine that has found an Alternative to just about everything except sex. And it's greater sexual freedom, of course, which has made jealousy such a dirty word. With fears of getting pregnant, poxed or fried in the hereafter largely out of the way, the one thing that could stand between you and a fine new love might be the tiresome unhappiness of the old one. So why can't they *stop* being unhappy, the spoil-sports?

Trouble is, as Miss Durbin points out, such godlike charity is mainly attainable by monks who have worked for years not just to overcome bad passions – like sexual jealousy – but good ones – like sexual love – as well. She'd been through it all: feeling guilty because she felt jealous, feeling free to go with a friend's husband because the friend serenely asserted 'we are far too close for that to matter' – and then finding the friend being worn away by the sheer effort of making it not matter.

She concluded that the old rule 'thou shalt not commit adultery' had simply been succeeded by a new one: 'thou shalt not feel jealous'; and if the old one was hard, the new one was downright impossible. 'What seems to be going by the board in the kind of thinking that attributes jealousy to personal insecurity or emotional immaturity or nursery school possessiveness is that love itself creates the conditions for anxiety.'

And the anxiety, I should have thought, would be more acute now than it's ever been. A senior wife in a polygamous situation, a traditional French wife or Victorian matron could look on any 'little sins of the flesh' with a fair degree of calm since she and the young love weren't supposed to be batting in the same league: witness the woman who gave not a fig for her husband's peccadillos, until one evening he had *dinner* with his mistress. Then she shot him. But no one can even say 'at least he'll always come back to me' these days: today's lay-by can always turn out to be tomorrow's permanent parking. It's ironic that jealousy should be outlawed at just the moment when you'd expect it to be violently on the increase.

And so, indeed, it is. At a recent chat-in for experts and advice columnists given by MIND, it was made clear that the place is simply crawling with it. There are women writing in to say: 'I know I'm silly but I can't stand him reading nudie mags,' plain sisters furiously jealous of pretty ones, older people feeling helpless jealousy (well disguised as disapproval) of the young and free; husbands who, like the parents of the sleeping beauty, fear a prick in every innocent sewing circle. And I was heartened that at least none of the advisers thought that the feeling could simply be made to go away.

That there were people who really didn't mind what their mates got up to, they didn't deny. But not all such complaisance, it seems, springs from 'so-long-as-you're-happy-dear' tolerance. There was this actor who had to sleep around 'for his art'; his wife hated it; when she finally managed to come to terms with it and stop minding, he stopped doing it. Again, I remember reading an article on open marriage which made me feel unbelievably mean and possessive – until the author happened to admit what a charge he got from the thought of other chaps' hands up his wife's skirt. And someone who has done advice phone-ins said more than once men have told her how they would have their wives pirouette on the dance floor with other men while they masturbated in the gallery.

That's not to say, of course, that there are no people who can come to terms with A. N. Other. Maybe there are plenty of people who don't care that much about sharing sex because sex isn't what matters to them. And I suppose there may be plenty who care *more* about sex than savage old primitives like me: in the sense of reckoning that it's the heat of the fire itself that's important, not what it does towards fusing two identities. Then, I daresay, the matter could become an almost gastronomic exchange, where one would be no more fed up that one's mate had laid a pretty girl than that he'd eaten a pleasant oyster.

The advisers were much more concerned, however, with fantasy jealousy: the consuming, obsessive passion that can sour every glance, every conversation, that can leave you racked and shaking like a fever. This is the real green-eyed monster: Othello *wrongly* suspecting Desdemona, men scared to let their wholly faithful (not to say totally boot-faced) wives down to the corner shop; women who go neurotically through their husbands' underwear in almost the sick hope of finding a bit of lipstick. This indeed is the suitable case for treatment.

It's the confusion with this sort of neurotic jealousy, I am sure, that makes it so easy to despise the legitimate misery of anyone who's being shortchanged. The green-eyed monster may be one of the nastiest beasts ever to gnaw on human vitals, but there's a blue-eyed monster who deserves a better break. If your elder brother is being taken to the theatre and you're not, you aren't neurotic to mind – of course you mind, any child would. If your lover is spending the evening in someone else's bed, he's not spending it in yours: why wouldn't you be upset?

The way to control the first sort of jealousy may be psychiatric help, but the cure for the second lies entirely elsewhere: in restraint or loyalty or reassurance or even a bit of discretion on the part of the person who's causing it. And if in the current climate that seems about as sensible as trying to cure the rain, we could at least stop blaming the people who end up wet.

Social Words for Social Workers II

Communicate: Speak.

Interrelate: Have a coffee with.

Interreaction: Have a coffee with and each pay for the other's.

Authoritative: Any theory you approve of.

Authoritarian: Any theory you disapprove of.

Structured environment: Probation Officer's phrase for the toughest detention centre going.

Job satisfaction: Attempts by management to ensure workers' co-operation without actually paying them any more.

Fantasy: Any interpretation of the facts not shared by the social worker.

The Media Gap

We hear a good deal about the rift between the two cultures and reading any article about the generations is like the speech before Harfleur: yet once more into the gap, dear friends. The one that gets mentioned less often is the invisible ha-ha between the communications world and the rest. By communications I mean plays, advertisements, newspapers, magazines, the lot – what we call media, which is a word no human being would naturally use.

I don't mean our harmless professional quirks, such as our conviction that *everybody* read yesterday's paper so that today's *Express* story kills tomorrow's one in the *Mail*, whereas *nobody* read the one last month so you can start all over again with that one. Nor does it mean the way we equate effort with importance, so that if you've stayed till midnight working on the central heating supplement or climbed the Himalayas to interview a lama, you think the world must be waiting.

No; I mean things inherent in the way we live which give us a different starting point in our way of thinking from other people. Take the simple fact that most of the media are run from London. We assume everybody at least *sees* the latest loony fashion on trips to town; we think of housing in terms of commuters or ratty Edwardian tenements, not half-empty mill towns; no amount of self-conscious forays down Coronation Street make us get the flavour of the provinces right. Half the time we're not even bothered by the difference. I met a man who'd done a survey on the nation's teeth: apparently in the south there are too many dentists chasing too few teeth and they cosset and preserve them as if they were the relics of St

Orifice. In the north there aren't so many dentists and they whip out the teeth with a wild abandon: she loves me, she loves me not, plenty more where that one came from. Dozens of interviewers and journalists pride themselves on having come *from* the north, of course (Keith Waterhouse's abrasive nostalgia in the *Daily Mirror*, like the smell of old broken beer bottles, is about the best thing going in journalism), but that isn't the same as actually living there.

Then there's money. It's not just that on the whole we have a lot for a short time instead of an even spread; it's that our ways of spending it are shared only by pools winners, prostitutes and sailors newly arrived in port. Living on expenses and perpetually short of time, we get to think taxis and restaurants are more normal than bus rides and breast of lamb. Since a successful announcer will never let himself think that he might be gone tomorrow, he tends to spend the money he earns today; it's quite a different outlook from the man whose income will go on being the same, whatever it is, for 20 years, let alone from those who were brought up never, never to sell the IBM shares.

There's a distortion, too, in knowing too much about something – and the cop on the corner is a case in point. Where the public sees a policeman, we see The Police. At a time when the police were complaining bitterly that the public hated them, a Government survey showed that in fact they were still quite popular; what had led to the over-plus of stories querying their behaviour was TV and newspaper consciousness of rough stuff by the cops in Chicago.

The world of news is the world of novelty, obviously; it's not enough to be on the bandwagon, you have to be driving it; and nowhere is this more so than with sex. Living in the midst of a fashion so dominating that even Lady Macbeth (in a castle in *Scotland*) is seen floating about with bare breasts. When they cannot even turn to a page of history without immediately finding a king who turned over two pages at once, we get it wrong about what is the norm.

I used to think that the chaotic sex lives of actors and photographers and writers were simply the result (as with travelling salesman) of the alibis being too good. But a psychologist finally convinced me it was a matter of temperament: the ability to become passionately interested in something for a short time and then drop it is their dominant characteristic. It is the same character defects that land communicators in the divorce court ('She and I just couldn't communicate somehow') that landed them their jobs in the first place.

The freedom of big city living is another distorting factor: Chelsea and Deptford have this in common, that it is those who don't fit anywhere else who end up there. Journalists and sociologists have agreed for years that the extended family is dead and even the nuclear one liable to fission at any moment – and then we suddenly read that three-quarters of nineteen-year-olds and 40 per cent of old-age pensioners live with their families – it makes you wonder if we're talking about the same nation.

I'm not saying our difference of viewpoint is always a bad thing; living in a tolerant world, the Press was ahead of the public on homosexual law reform, and if we've extended our own freemasonry so that it's no longer respectable to run down a man for colour or accent, so much the better. The aerial view may well tell you more about a farm's layout and possibilities than you'd find out down among the cowsheds.

But it isn't the same. And this means that if you do feel totally out of step with what the world seems to be thinking, you needn't take too much notice. The tides may be flowing the way the stage and the Press and TV say they are, or they may not. But we are no more typical than the first TV performers, who had to wear gold eyelids and blue lips for the camera.

Husband-Swapping

Every time I see a headline about wife-swapping I read on eagerly; but it always turns out to be swapping just for the night. And where's the percentage in that?

Maybe I'm lucky, but I've never had much urge to change beds. Almost all my problems, however, could be solved by a little daylight robbery of other people's chaps, offering my own in exchange. The other day I had a marvellous moan with another wife whose writer husband works at home. That is, he (like mine) works for about twenty minutes, and then some plumber, Jehovah's Witness or man coming to fail to mend the cooker disturbs the concentration for the day.

Mine rushes out to greet this stream of artisans, hers stays behind closed doors and suffers; but it comes to much the same thing; his suffering can be felt all over the house if he so much as hears the crunch of Witness on gravel. If only, we said wistfully, we could change them over: mine wouldn't mind *her* anti-rot squad, hers would scarcely notice anyone else's electricians, any more than one notices the noise of anonymous cars and trains. It would be perfect.

There are girls, I suspect, who would like to commit the ultimate P. G. Wodehouse crime of pinching my cook (I mean the one I'm married to). And I have a secret yearning for this man who said, quite casually, mind you, 'When I'm cleaning pans.' All that Brillo is not gold, but even to have my afternoon off with such a man!

And on Monday I was greeted by a bleary-eyed friend who had, as usual, been up by six; her husband was once a jockey and can never really understand that people, unlike horses, haven't necessarily got the bloat if they don't feel like exercising in the grey dawn. But he cuts the grass three times a week whereas in our house the lawnmower is a conversation piece. (The conversation goes 'Will you be cutting the grass?' 'No.') We both agreed it would be marvellous if my chaos could mop up some of the super spare energy that she finds so exhausting; 'though mind you,' she said, 'if I got together with yours, we'd never do anything at all. It would,' she sighed, 'be wonderful.'

We all have our illusions: I would love to try being married to someone who didn't discover his trousers needed pressing just twenty minutes before visitors are due – or at least one who doesn't sit pathetically in the drawing-room in his underpants while the pressing goes on; he, for his part, no doubt sometimes fancies being married to the kind of wife who actually goes looking for trouble (i.e. unpressed trousers) in other people's wardrobes.

But there could be snags. I have this methodical friend whose wife I generally envy (at college he thought he won our philosophical arguments by force of reason; actually it was the way he straightened cushions between sentences that put me off my stroke). But how would such a person feel about the suitcase of old clothes I've left in the hall for four months? I never tried him out for tolerance. And what would happen to my illusion that I am a force for order in the home if I wasn't married to the only man north of the Tiber who is even untidier than I am?

Again, every married couple consists of one Accelerator and one Brake. The high-speed wife resents being dragged home by a pin-striped commuter intent on tomorrow's trains, and thinks she'd do better swapping with the weary helpmeet of the Life and Soul, the man who will never go home while there is one man, woman or glass of anything not yet drunk. But what would become of her image of herself as a gaiety girl if she was suddenly the one who had to haul her man home? How, indeed, would old steady really feel, if she was not dragged out to have a good time once in a while?

Only a bit of judicious switching would tell us. And since we don't all have exactly the right neighbours for a controlled test (like the poor chap in the paper recently who called off the wife-swap because his swop had her leg in plaster), we need a national exchange register: where you could apply for someone who is the exact opposite of your own spouse. Or, perhaps even more revealing, the one who is like yours only worse – an especially good exercise for those whose husbands are only *fairly* pre-occupied executives, *nearly* full-time alcoholics, *almost* certifiable, monks *manqué* but not quite.

And who knows, we might find we came gratefully back to our own mates simply because we know how to cope with them. We might even find that other people's grumbles were worse than our own – why, some women even have to put up with *wife-swapping*.

A-Work and B-Work

Something which a perfectly serious professor said the other day has made me realise at last why All Working Together is and will remain no more than a sticky smear round the mouths of honey-sucking politicians.

What he said (he trades under the name of Prof. Maurice Peston) was that he'd seen figures to show that it's not true that the British working man works any less hard than the dawn-rising Dane or conscientious Kraut: he works as hard as any. When, that is, he is actually working. The only snag is that he doesn't seem keen to do it for more than a couple of hours a day.

Since writers to *The Times* are always pointing out that they, too, count as working men, and since it's hardly likely that those higher up the ladder, with their infinitely greater scope, would work any more hours than the manual worker, the question then remains for us all: if we only work two hours a day, what is it we are doing the rest of the time?

Suppose we call the work which people do in those two hours – and which they think, of course, they do all the time – the A-work. A-work is actually hitting the sheet metal or the typewriter keys, cutting into cloth or patients, heaving hay into heaps, telephoning the Minister saying it's impossible, or swapping a packet of tobacco and 30p for a pound note. It's unlikely that your A-work offends anyone much (demarcation disputes aside); everyone understands that bakers must knead bread, cops grab robbers round the ankles, farmers reach their sensitive experienced hands towards the o'erflowing udders of cows to adjust the milking machinery.

Then everything else you do in working hours becomes the B-work. This includes lawyers leaning against one another's desks recalling the case of Rex *v.* Blockett, gardeners walking to the other end of the row to see if that was where they left the dibber, writers zooming toy cars across their desks to stimulate inspiration, and executives dropping in on their subordinates to pass the time of day, good human relations being the (not well kept) 'secret' of successful management. It is the time taken climbing down the crane to fetch the spanner, it is saying 'I'll have a word with him,' it is filling up the form, it is the site foreman saying to the contractor, 'It says here two by four, do you really mean three and seven eighths or what?'

The point being that you can't say all this *isn't* work, in the sense that there is any reasonable way of bounding straight into the A-work without it. But it's this, I'm sure, which causes most of the friction, because nobody ever really understands anyone's B-work but their own.

Why do middle-class ladies get into such a froth over the help having a cup of tea? They don't really believe she's got no right to sit down for five minutes. People working on a factory bench imagine that salesmen spend their entire time eating expensive lunches, which is what they find so maddening; few bosses can stand seeing a secretary reading a newspaper even when they honestly believe it's a good idea for her to keep up with current events.

What happened during the three-day week was that everyone had a rotten time cutting down on their B-work and doing only the A; and the moral is of such bottomless embarrassment to us all that we've been doing our best to forget about it ever since.

It's probably an illusion that some jobs consist of B-work alone. An historian I know said his old mates from Liverpool couldn't ever understand how anyone would pay him real money just for looking at books. One astringent news editor is apt to silence reporters who gripe about staying up nights rewriting copy or getting stranded in Wigan with the words, 'It's still better than going to work' – to him, plainly, work is definable and nasty and journalism isn't it.

The best careers advice given to the young (at least to boys; girls' schools can spot a snag to it) is 'Find out what you like doing best and get someone to pay you for doing it'; but it's a moot point whether it then ceases to be work at all, or whether it simply seems to have an extra high B-work content.

What's certain is that you don't get the right pegs into the right holes by looking at the work – the A-work – alone. It's old hat that people don't on the whole work for money (or why would the best paid, e.g. motor workers, be the ones to be forever on strike); management courses teach an elaborate structures of incentives which include things like approval of colleagues and whether people sneer in the street or kiss your hem with some such words as, 'Oh, *thank* you, doctor.' But the crucial question of how you get through all those hours remains the hardest to assess.

This is why books that do describe the entire scene are so compelling: James Herriot's vet books, for example, are about driving over bumpy roads, looking for a long time at a sunset, drinking with farmers, setting out at night in pyjamas to seek out a sick sheep halfway up a frozen fell; absolutely none of which would be covered by a job description of what he might actually do to an unwell animal.

The day may come when advertisements appear saying 'Oaklined office peopled by Wykehamists: opera spoken about, chess played; pace of life, three revs per hour; a liking for smooth paper and well pressed trousers an asset.' Or perhaps, 'Brown Rover; aggressive boss welcomes personality clashes, restless time-scheme; chance to impress sodden and unkind Midlanders with southern sophistication. Suit greying advertising executive seeking illusion of Reality.' It could come out at interview, perhaps, that the first was in the Treasury and the second in the sale of machine tools; but that, it would be recognised, would be entirely secondary.

Games of Seven

Seven Ages of Scepticism

If you eat up your carrots, you'll be able to see in the dark.
Oh go on, you can tell *me!* I won't breathe a word to a soul.
We can't have a mature relationship if you won't.
Rinso banishes washday blues.
Poor Charles, his first wife was so unspeakably neurotic.
It's lovely, big grounds, only forty inmates, you'll love it.
Goodness, you'll be as right as rain in a day or two.

Seven ways not to start

But you promised!
I only said . . .
If you'd been listening, you'd have realised . . .
But *Mummy*!
Darling, I don't know how you're going to take this . . .
We like it, of course, BUT . . .
May I tell my story about . . .

Seven very bad signs

Steak knives laid with liver and bacon.
Muzak in the middle of the flight.
The smell of tomcat in an empty house – hides smell of dry rot.
Brown envelopes with a transparent window.
The cat disdaining the fish you've just eaten.
The glance of a shopgirl measuring your stomach.
Six dog leads in the hall.

We are the Natives Now

The trouble with warm weather is the way it brings out foreigners. I react to them as hay fever victims do to pollen; and the tourist count just now is abnormally high.

Like hay fever, it's an allergic reaction: that's to say, it's what I do to myself that causes the damage. They themselves are all right.

I like the Americans with their clean mackintoshes and hopeful expressions and the checked trousers that prove they're on vacation; I admire the rippling muscles of the Italians (even if they do sometimes spoil it by speaking with a strong cockney accent), and though I loathe the way the French talk across you as if you aren't there (the French in this century, like the Britons in the last, travelling mainly for the pleasure of despising what they see), there's always a mean pleasure to be got from addressing them in French and showing you understood what they were saying – a possibility that never seems to cross their minds.

But once the summer visitors arrive, I can't behave naturally. Just as, waitressing in California, I resisted the urge to stick a pickle-fork in the neck of some rude and overfed brat because he might one day wind up President and refuse aid to the British, so I can't do a thing without wondering what the visitors will think.

If I pick my teeth in the street, they'll think British women pick their teeth. If they shove me out of the way in a queue, I smile gamely to show them what a tolerant lot we are. I lean over their maps and muddle them with instructions lest they should ever think the Brits aren't friendly and forthcoming.

And that's only the strangers. The ones one knows are even worse. First there's the little note saying they'll be at the St Raucous Hotel, please ring 23 June; then there are the endless conversations with the desk clerk, who, since it's a London Hotel, is Swiss or Italian and doesn't speak a word of English; finally they turn up an hour and a half early for dinner because they were told you can't get taxis after six, or three hours late because they thought you meant *any* time this evening.

And they are never one's own dear foreign friends either, but their stodgy au pair daughters, their slick business uncles, their sisters and their cousins whom they reckon on by dozens. . . . Never Stay With An Extended Family ought to be printed into the passport of every travelling Briton.

Presumably there are more of them around this summer because the falling pound makes Britain cheap, and tourism is about our only booming industry. But seeing ourselves through their eyes isn't pleasant. For every one Norwegian who enthuses about us as 'warm-hearted southerners', there seem to be two Japanese who see one as a cross between a chateau-bottled bottle and a Sabine woman, three Americans radiating friendly pity (I don't doubt by now their guide books recommend the *muy tipico* British banger and say we're a proud, shy, retiring people) and at least one Frenchman who stabs one in the chest with a bony finger and asks why we were two months late with the reinforcements for the resistance at Vercors.

It's this feeling of being on the mat for one's whole nation that I find so trying. I want to dance about and say look, *I* didn't put up Centre Point, it wasn't *me* that shot your god-dam General, don't blame *me* for the brake that came off your Triumph; all I'm doing is sitting up straight not biting my nails cooking you the only English dish I know. I'm doing my best, I only work here, don't pick on me.

And the real reason they make me feel so rotten is that of course they're right, in a way. We all talk, all the time, of 'they' – they the trade unions, they the beastly capitalists, they the people who don't work hard any more – but who are 'they'?

My theory about what's wrong with Britain, if you happen to want to know, is that we've got Dutch Elm Disease – as you will appreciate if you know how the disease works. It isn't the beetle that does the damage, nor yet the fungus infection that it carries; it's the tree itself which, to protect itself, cuts off supplies to any leaf which the fungus hits – to any twig, any branch – and at last to the trunk, which kills it.

I've sat at a union meeting asking for a rise (because of inflation, of which we disapprove) and in a board room agreeing to put up prices (because of inflation, of which we disapprove) – so who *is* inflation, if it isn't me? Who doesn't work hard enough, drinks too much, takes affluence for granted? You mean *me*?

No wonder I resent the frogs and wogs and yanks and wops and krauts and goddam limeys – no, hold it, that's me – who remind me that *L'état c'est moi*; and I bet Louis XIV was being made to squirm by some tactless British Ambassador when he said it. Never mind; in the autumn, unlike my other troubles, they will all go away.

Panel Games

'The panel of judges in the *News of the World* Sins of the Seventies contest were at first divided in their choice. Half voted for Murder, half for Rape, with only Lady Bathworthy, our leading lady novelist, opting for Adultery; she thought it must be the deadliest because it was the most tempting, but was talked out of it by the chairman.

'Supporters of the other sins stuck to their guns, however, Lord Porn maintaining that Rape was a pathological crime and so didn't count, while Tony Harker insisted that many, indeed most, of his best friends were murderers. The deadlock was only resolved by abandoning both sins and turning to second choices: rejected were Treason (too political), Gluttony (unlikely to please the paper's advertisers) and Putting Used Matches Back in the Box; though infuriating to women and so likely to spoil the serenity of the British home, it hardly rated in this context *above* adultery. After fourteen hours' debate the judges, considering that an environmental sin would be the most apt for the decade, chose Parking On a Double Yellow Line as the winner, with a special mention for Being Drunk in Charge of a Pram.'

The only unlikely bit in all that is the judges getting through in a mere fourteen hours: choosing the winner in a competition can take days, it can take weeks. And whether it is to choose Miss Yoghourt 1971, a slogan for sixth forms or a Racehorse Most Likely to Sire a Derby Winner, the judging follows much the same pattern. You start hopefully, thinking that your favourite may win the contest; in an inconceivably short time you only want to block the chances of the one you hate most. Any tea-set, poem or colour-scheme that is original enough to delight some will be striking enough to revolt the others, so if the votes are cast by marking (out of ten, say) you can be certain the one you love will not come up: however new the maths, six sevens are still more than three tens and three twos. Indeed, any honest panel is bound to be split clean down the middle at some point; nothing could be more suspicious than a set of judges all bunched around one viewpoint, like witches round a moorland fire.

It is all very disillusioning. To start with, it's a salutary shock that other people's views can be so totally opposed to one's own – as I found out for the first time at a hairstyle contest where all the prizes were going to heaps of pink candy floss in the form of the Eiffel Tower, and I do mean pink. It's upsetting, as with crowds and committees, to see how the wind of opinion can veer – people change their minds so fast that an entry which gets highest marks at stage 1 can get no marks at all at stage 2.

Some commercial firms openly take 'geographical balance' into account – those women who write and say 'Why no winner from Scotland?' don't know the harm they do. No wonder there are various sets of Queensberry rules for things like design and literary contests, so that the name and address are separate from the entry itself, and you don't know you're turning down Graham Greene.

In practice, there are several roads to a decision. Just as in the old 'Any Questions?' the question-master would say firmly 'The team is agreed that on the one hand and on the other hand,' so a forceful chairman just says, 'That's agreed, then' the first time there's a lull in the fighting, and hopes everyone will be too tired or too cowed to reopen fire. Or he can deliberately keep them in until it becomes, as the man said of committees, a victory for the man with the strongest bladder. He can set up an intensely complicated, weighted, mathematical voting system, and sweep to a finish while the panel are still counting it out on their fingers. And sometimes a deadlock is broken by the discovery of some overlooked entry under the table, which strikes everyone with a happy freshness; the chairman can clinch the deal before they've time to get tired of that one too.

Sometimes a Great Name has been brought in to lend tone to what would otherwise be an unseemly wrangle between, say, manufacturers of fizzy drinks, and he may settle matters by waking up halfway through, asserting his choice, and saying he will, of course, withdraw his Name if there is any nonsense about a majority decision. And when the organisers are really old hands they let the judges blow themselves out in any way that pleases them, and then explain later (in case anyone remembers what *was* decided) that the top ten entries had to be disqualified for technical reasons: the contester lived outside the sterling area, would have been the eleventh successful contestant from Morecambe Bay that year, was the chairman's niece, was not the chairman's niece, was a pensioner of ninety-seven and would have looked awful in the publicity photographs for a Honeymoon Holiday in the Bahamas for Two.

When you think of the hazard of even getting on to a short list, it seems even more amazing that there are certain people who win the kind of competition you get on the back of cornflake packets over and over again – every year you read storie about some woman who has won ten fridges and thirty-two colour TV sets. Win them they do – and the roulette ball *can* come up red seventeen times running. But it doesn't do to expect too much of the game. When a man starts playing roulette on a system (as Dornford Yates' Berry said) it's time to start praying for his soul.

The Decent Inn of Death

Notice boards tell you a lot. On the board at St Christopher's there's a notice about a party; a fashion show; the times of chapel services; and the announcement of the births of a first baby to two different couples: 'All six are doing well.' It makes you understand how one patient said she liked the place: 'Where I was before, they stick you away in a corner with an oxygen cylinder: here there's a bit of life.'

Which is an odd way to describe a place to which patients come only when other outfits have failed with them: when families can't cope or hospitals can't keep the pain under. They have cancer or motor neurone disease and most of them aren't expected to get better. Or, rather, survive – 'get better' they certainly do (quite apart from the few, every year, who confound the doctors and make it home again for good).

As anyone who has ever fallen foul of an airport, a conventional hospital or a bad restaurant knows, misery is made up of little things – so St Christopher's Hospice is meticulous about little things, such as the matron or doctor getting into the ambulance to welcome a new patient; or making it quite clear that dogs can come to visit ('actually we had a baby elephant in the garden last week and it didn't go upstairs only because it was apparently too tired to get into the lift'); or telling any patient who feels well enough to go home for a spell that they can come back at a moment's notice if they feel they're slipping; or forbidding visiting on Mondays 'so that families can do the washing or get drunk without feeling guilty'.

There's no X-ray, no operating theatre, no pathology lab – but there's a team of outriders who help people in the area cope at home with badly smitten patients; there's a clubroom for the families of dying people who have to be helped with the sick person's anger: 'Anger's a component of any terminal illness – any illness as a matter of fact; it's sad if you turn on the person closest to you; we have to explain to the wife that it's because he feels safe enough to take it out on you – it'll pass; hold on tight.'

The bereaved need to be able to talk and talk – everyone else is probably shutting them up and telling them Not to Brood. And later on, there are a few who need someone else to tell them that it's all right to stop grieving – that they can start to live their lives again.

To keep the feel of the place normal the Hospice has set up an old people's wing on one hand, and a nursery for staff children on the other – presumably one of the reasons they've never had to have an agency nurse in the place. In addition, they have ninety students a year on four-week courses (who also do ward duties) and something like 2,000 day visitors like me (who don't).

Some of them are pretty starry-eyed: one American was taking in a tray to a patient and was casually told 'I'm not eating that – I'm dying!' She bubbled back to the kitchen: 'It's true! They really do get relaxed about it!' 'Maybe so,' said the cook, 'but what she actually said was "I'm dieting"– you've got the wrong tray.'

Somehow the idea of a cheerful place in which people die has the synthetic, jarring sound of something out of *The Loved One*, a 'brave face' cosmetically plastered over suffering; Dr Cicely Saunders, who started the place, is as hostile to the idea of a Fun Death as she is to thickly pious people who tell her it's a privilege to work with the dying. 'It's *hard*,' she says, 'it *hurts*.'

This remarkable woman was a nurse and an Oxford PPE before she became determined to do something about the wretched habits of big, busy hospitals 'where everyone tiptoes past the bed and the dying soon learn to pretend to be asleep'. In the space of a year or two she had several people close to her die, including her father: 'I got my bereavements very muddled up at one point.' When she said she wanted to help people with severe cancer, a friend told her she'd never do it as a nurse: 'Very well then,' she said, 'I'll become a doctor.' And did.

The job, she reckons, is twofold: to ease pain, and to help people who aren't going to recover to come to terms with it.

You can do a lot of things about pain, from hitting the sufferer on the head with a mallet, to pouring half the whisky into the wound and half into the cowboy; 'my father,' said Dr West, the Deputy Director, 'died happy on brandy and codeine.' But the trouble with today's Brompton cocktails – usually a mixture of largactil and morphine or heroin – is that if you need to step up the pain-killing, you step up the sedative side, and vice versa; at the Hospice they have subtler strings to their bows.

'Pain's physical, social, mental and spiritual – you have to work out which is which and treat the right one. People get hooked on clock-watching for pain.' They have tales of people brought in under dope who needed very little once they were certain they'd get relief when they needed it. That way, they could be clear-headed enough, in the end, to know the truth.

'Do you always tell them?' I asked. 'We never lie to them,' Dr West said. 'We don't force it on them either. Quite often the families, in the first shock of knowing, have said "You mustn't tell" – and then there's been an intolerable barrier: one man said "I couldn't think what had gone wrong with my marriage." ' And one of the nurses said 'It's *always* a relief when they know. "Will I die?" one woman asked, and was told, yes. "Will you keep me?" "Of course." "Do I have to eat?" "No." "Then I can rest." '

What about religion? 'I came here to die,' sighed one woman, 'and I've prayed; but I haven't died and praying's just as boring as it always was.' Dr Saunders is C of E, but worked for years at St Joseph's, which is nuns; and Dr West was a medical missionary in Nigeria. 'The ones who find it hardest are those who had a conventional religion and now are face to face with reality,' he says, 'but the really religious often seem to be appallingly tested before they go.'

An American outfit started out to set up a secular version of St Christopher's and was surprised to find that 80 per cent of the people it recruited were, in fact, religious; it's possible that, though each man's death is his own, only those who do believe there's something beyond can take the weight of other people's, day after day.

In our current straits, it's hardly likely that Hospices will spring up like mushrooms – though there are half a dozen such places here and there. So the big question is: how much of all this can be passed on?

Certainly their expertise in the control of pain is a speciality that can be respected like any other; and the idea's spreading that 'we can't cure you' doesn't have to mean the same thing as 'we can't do anything for you': those last few weeks can be infinitely precious: compare the fantasy of the teenager 'half in love with easeful death' who thinks 'If I'd only a week to live' – wine, women and song – with what actually happens if you've only a week to live: they can hardly be bothered to pass your spectacles half the time.

'There's a *lot* we could do,' said a nurse from a teaching hospital who was going round when I was. 'We put screens round the dying, never tell the other patients – it's supposed not to alarm them, but it does the opposite of course.' Plainly the idea of caring more for how a patient – or his family – feel about the disease is a ground swell that's sweeping all the shores of medicine.

There's one drawback I see no way round: at St Christopher's nobody has to be cajoled into treatment, forced to eat, put through it in the interests of a cure – but how would a general hospital ever get it right about when to let the patient off the effort? At least there's one comfort, though: the systems of medicine we have here, however rickety, at least don't inspire doctors to go on hopelessly operating and injecting and radiating lest they be sued by the bereaved, as they do in the States – and where it's free, the family don't feel they *must* insist on a treatment lest they feel they've guiltily let themselves off paying the money.

'Hope,' Dr Saunders says, 'there's always hope. Even if you can't hope for a cure, you can hope for a good night, or to see your daughter's wedding, or to enjoy a meal.'

Or you can hope, with Chesterton,

. . . to see undrugged in evening
light the decent inn of death.
For there are good things yet to hear
and good things to be seen
Before we go to paradise by way of
Kensal Green.

The Uses of Illiteracy

One thing at least is over for a year: those demoralising lists of what the Great and Good liked best to read in the year just ended. Sir Marcus Thinktank loved the sensitive delineation of menopausal awakening in the new Doris O'Drabble; Petal Bravo was impressed by the Rights of Microbes: Is There Intelligent Life on Man?; while the Frayns and Brains have been knocked sideways by a biography of Santarolarola, whose thirteenth-century mystic writings are available only in Russian.

Am I the only moron to feel so put down by all this literacy? They actually asked me to do it once; easy, I said, I've only read one new book this year; an embarrassed titter and I wasn't asked again. It's particularly bad for those of us who read slowly: I don't actually mouth the words as I go, but there'd certainly be time for it if I did; at that speed, you think twice before you start on 400-page biographies, however revealing. The only advantage of it is that you never need *re*-read anything, because it all stays with you; I think it's unreasonable of the family to expect me to remember films, too, since I take in those at the same speed as everyone else.

Books do furnish a room, of course, and the earnest market researcher would no doubt think I'm a lot more literate than I am, as she checked her list: Are there one/five/more than five books in the house? How many are upside down/reference works/about Princess Anne? But the books about aeroplanes and the thrillers aren't mine, and the ponderous tomes on the history of PT, mating rituals in the Tobriand Islands or new methods of teaching French to the handicapped are there simply because they've been sent by the publishers and I'm too brainwashed by education to chuck them in the dustbin. Even the ones I do hopefully buy to improve my mind – things like Roznak's *Making of a Counter Culture* or *The Greening of America* (which always makes me think there must be some boisterous poet down under known as the Browning of Australia) – these are apt simply to sit on the shelves, as if by some process of osmosis I will somehow absorb their contents without actually reading them.

And it's not as if I hadn't been properly steeped in Eng. Lit.; but that's no automatic passport to a booksy heaven. Not if I could get a perfectly reasonable degree in Eng. Lit. at a good university without having read one word of Joyce's *Ulysses* or Macauley or Proust or Malory or Scott or Thackeray or *Cranford* or *Pamela* or the *Religio Medici* or any American author whatsoever – and I'm not prepared to say which of these gaps (if any) I've filled in since.

I doubt anyway whether the booksy world is quite the Cloud Nine it thinks it is. My regard for The Novel, never high, sank several notches on learning that all the boy-meets-girl merchants turned cheerfully to boy-meets-boy, girl-meets-girl and meaningful-confrontations-in-brothels-following-the-atom-holocaust when their publishers told them this was now what the market wanted.

Can the book trade conceivably know what it is doing if it gets out just under a hundred books *a day* – well over 35,000 titles a year? Surely even the Secret of the Universe could hardly take 2,450 million words.

And as for the best seller lists, being on one for several weeks I suppose entitles me to sneer at them without being accused of envy; when I was on them with a book that had only *printed* 12,000 a friend was not, though his book had *sold* 120,000 – only his was about kitchen gardens so it didn't count. When my husband had to get hold of a copy of *The Bermuda Triangle* because he was reviewing the work which demolished the theory, he found it was out of print and unobtainable – but still selling, the lists said, in the top ten.

I'm not actually suggesting that book production simply ceases for a year or two to let me catch up. But I do wish the book pages would give a lot more Facts From Books for those of us who aren't even going to pretend to read them. It would help if TV could stop at ten; they could bring down the price of waterproof torches to make it easier to read in the bath; and the next time some newcomer to novel-writing confesses shyly to the reporters (as one did the other day) that she's starting on a trilogy, each third of which will be 500 pages long, she should be very gently led away, given a packet of sandwiches and a one-way ticket for Outer Mongolia. Though even that wouldn't work, I suppose, if she wrote her blasted memoirs on return.

Are They Old Enough to say 'No'?

Some time ago one trendy parson hit the headlines by recommending the age of consent to be brought down; as it was Honest John Robinson I decided, like Elinor Dashwood, not to pay him the compliment of rational opposition. But now that Timothy Beaumont has also nailed his dog-collar to this particular mast, I have a great fear that Sex before Sixteen may become one of those causes, like Vietnam or the Oz trial, that no parson who wants to be on the side of Youth will dare to take the opposite line from them.

It so happened that the very week that Honest John blew his top I was listening to a policeman from the Midlands lecturing trainees on the problems of prostitution. One of the trickiest, he said, was the young girl of 13 or 14 who had a row with her family, slammed out of the house and showed up in a doubtful café looking for a taste of life. She would be scooped up almost at once and passed like stolen goods from one protector to another, so that she didn't stay more than two days with any one. 'If we don't get that girl back in ten days or so,' he said, 'it's often too late, she's on the game for good.'

It was not quite the innocent cleric's view of two sweet young things rubbing noses in a flowery field; but I don't have much doubt in which scene the law is more important.

It's always hard, of course, to get people to think clearly about the usefulness of law. When the Latey Committee (me included) recommended that parental consent to marriage shouldn't be needed after 18, we got widely ticked off for having 'said that people should marry at 18'. We didn't say anything of the sort, of course: what we said was that after 18 or so the legal parental veto doesn't work.

Where there's a good relationship, what the parents think counts, law or no law; where there isn't, people of that age either ignore or evade what's often a wrongheaded prohibition anyway. Similarly what's at issue here is *not* whether every 15-year-old found under a hedge with another 15-year-old has actually done anything so frightful; but whether we do or don't need a law to stop older predatory people exploiting the inexperience of very young girls – or boys, for that matter.

One tends to forget, I think, now that far more people are doing their own thing younger and with less guilt, that good old-fashioned exploitation hasn't just gone away. Older and dominating men still do use their experience to back young girls into a psychological corner. People still do get young girls on the game. Rape remains an extremely difficult crime to prove, partly, of course, because there is such an area of doubt in a good many tussles; but also because it's so hard to get it taken seriously – and there's even a school of 'victim psychology' which tries to suggest that nobody gets raped who doesn't want to be.

Likewise living on immoral earnings – poncing – is a very tricky charge to make stick: you practically have to catch the girl in the act of handing over the cash. When the age of consent went up to 16 in 1885 it was to protect youngsters from exploitation, and there isn't any other protection that covers the same ground.

Ah, but youngsters nowadays are so clear-eyed, so sophisticated, so able to make their own decisions these days . . . well, *are* they? Some of them; all right, some of them. But the postbags of the advice columnists haven't suddenly emptied of letters from the young: far from it. Most of them are simply more bewildered younger; what used to be 'Should I let my boyfriend kiss me' at 17 is now 'Should I let him sleep with me?' at 16. They are spectacularly bad at birth control: 'They act as if they're using it but they aren't,' as one social worker put it; and no one has yet started saying that pregnancies and abortions are just what the teenager needs.

And grown-up opinion surely ought to be a bit behind what the kids want to do: it really must not add its weight to the pressures that make a girl feel she *ought* to go and sleep with someone. In the days when all respectable girls were supposed to be virgins, a good many of them weren't, but at least you could suppose that the non-virgins had followed the devices and desires of their own hearts; in the current climate girls may go to bed with boys simply to do what the others are doing.

I remember, though not with much pleasure, my first kiss: I thought it was awful not to have been kissed at 16; the deed was done by a salivary stranger during a kissing game at a party: not only no feeling for the chap, but no pleasure even in the kiss itself. It horrifies me to think there may now be girls getting no more than that out of their first bedding.

There's just one argument which I doubt if either of the reverend gentlemen would advance, but which we may as well tackle while we're at it. Isn't it rather hard on some poor chap who didn't know she was under age? Honest, m'lud, she *looked* 17. . . .

Well, no, as a matter of fact, it bloody well isn't. If a man is sailing into bed with a girl without knowing enough about her or her family, or whether she's at school, about her home or lack of it to know whether she is or isn't lying about her age, how much idea is *he* going to have about whether he's doing her any harm or not? If we have to give someone the benefit of the doubt, I don't think we can save it for the man who makes passes at parties. Not while there's any doubt at all as to whether the 14-year-old in the new eye make-up really knows what she's doing.

Where the Money Goes II

To: Chief Accountant
From: Assistant Editor

As you suggested, I have questioned Madden about the expenses for his Oxbridge trip; he agrees that £380 2*s.* 10*d.* for one night is unusually high. Taxi (15*s.*) and porter (7*s.* 6*d.*) – twice – were expenses apparently necessitated by the large number of books he had with him, including a four-volume history of the Hanseatic League which he was reviewing for a Third Programme symposium. He insists that as these outside appearances help to get the paper's 'names' more widely known, it is not inappropriate to lay this charge to us.

The hired car (£7 7*s.*) was laid on for the purpose of pursuing into the countryside one of his interviewees, who apparently has a reputation for taking flight on a bicycle at the approach of the Press. His hotel bill (£10 16*s.*) and bill for 'food' (£12 17*s.* 6*d.*) are admittedly high, but I see no way of querying it without calling him a liar to his face.

The final item, 'broken glass £340', was incurred during a student demonstration in his hotel. Madden, dressing as he does, was understandably mistaken by the management for one of the ringleaders. The exuberance of the protest had demolished a small conservatory for which the manager pressed for payment; to refuse, Madden felt, would label our paper a fascist rag in the eyes of the students and do untold harm to future circulation. He accordingly paid up, and was chaired enthusiastically to the nearest pub by the students, where, I gather, he got stuck with the bill again (£14 8*s.* 10*d.*). The item of 3*s.* 6*d.* for milk on the train I have disallowed.

Hypocrisy For Today

Few things cheer one more on a bad day than thinking about the depravity of one's ancestors. Look at them, burning witches, sending little boys up chimneys; fifty lashes, Mr Christian, and we are taking off your toenails in the name of the Father, the Son and the Holy Ghost. Sister Susie sewed shirts for sixpence a day while the Bishop droned on about heavenly love. We may have our problems too, but at least we aren't hypocritical about them.

Or maybe thinking we're *not* hypocritical is our biggest hypocrisy; for actually there seems to be plenty about. And I don't mean just hangover hypocrisy of the traditional sort – 'charitable' ladies who pay £25 for the tickets to the ball and £250 for the dress they wear to it. There's a fresh new set for progressives, too.

We're supposed to have stopped being hypocritical about sex; and I suppose there are fewer chaps who visit a mistress on Tuesdays and Thursdays while denouncing sin on Sundays, fewer sex-starved bachelors beating little boys' bottoms in boarding schools. But we are just as good at scapegoating the woman who Pays the Price – only nowadays it isn't the fallen woman with the shameful bundle, it's the wife he left behind him. Look how magazines and interviews concentrate on the successful current ménage; look how eager we all are to be reassured that any wife who was abandoned must have been unfaithful or frigid – or at least given to saying 'No thanks, I won't have a drink, I'll have a sip or two of my husband's.'

Newly divorced people are always saying 'the children have taken it awfully well' or 'My boys just love Ann'; yet Brenda

Maddox' book, *The Half-Parent: Living with Other People's Children*, has revealed a seething pit of hate and unhappiness. Where's the wicked stepmother in our mythology? I'd say we were no keener to talk about the casualties of freedom than ye ole mother church was to talk about the casualties of restraint.

Of course, hypocrisy is often just a desperate attempt to bridge the gap between what you aspire to and what you are: moral costume jewellery, to kid your friends and with any luck yourself, that you're not doing so badly after all. Politically, this means you can live in a ten-bedroomed house with £200 chairs and wall-to-wall whisky at the weekends, but so long as you wear jeans and not a tweed skirt you can denounce the middle classes with all the gritty passion of a starving ditchdigger.

You must not, of course, spend any of the money on your children's schooling (electronic jigsaws and language trips to Switzerland are OK). This sort of hypocrisy peaked, I suppose, in Vanessa Redgrave's statement that it was all right for her to send her child to a private school since it was an uncle not her that was actually paying.

Prating equality, but paying to go private is standard: the NUT, so in favour of State education, has a private medical insurance plan for its members, while the MPU doctors, so dedicated to the NHS, have a private educational insurance scheme.

But the double think doesn't stop there: if the Labour Party really cared about equality it would tackle the fee-paying sector *first*, and leave the direct grant schools to the last – after all they do hoist some poor children to the level of the privileged; that Labour is doing it the other way round proves that the object of the exercise is to make them feel warmly egalitarian, not actually to change much.

We aren't over the old hypocrisy about language, either.

When the BBC a few years ago hauled a few families up to London to ask them what they disliked on the telly, they were amazed that the families scarcely worried about the violence, hardly more about sex, but went on and on and *on* about the vile language. They maybe weren't in the van of modern thinking, but it wouldn't have made much difference if they had been.

Again, look at the reaction to the marital dust-ups of Harold Pinter. Most of Fleet Street was far more shocked by what Vivien Merchant *said* than about anything Lady Antonia Fraser might have *done*: jealousy is very unprogressive. We know these things go on, of course, but one doesn't talk about them.

And there's a whole area, not just of forbidden words but of taboo ideas, a refusal to look any fact in the face that might conceivably rock one's theology. There was a splendid instance at a recent conference on dyslexia, one form of which is caused – if I may over-simplify – by the bits of your brain being assembled in an unusual order, right cutting across left and so forth. Plainly, this is not something your foul family can have done to you environmentally; yet one woman got up and said, 'I don't *want* to believe it's genetic. . . .' Why not? Because 'genetic' is a dirty word that implies all babes are not born equal Never mind that the child's trouble would have to be properly recognised if he was to get anything like an equal start.

Shaw said that you never found an Englishman doing anything except on principle; he enslaves you on imperialistic principles, he starves you on economic principles . . . it hasn't changed. It's just that now the dustsheet under which we hide what we are really up to is labelled liberty, equality, fraternity. Oh, and don't let's forget 'self-fulfilment' – that covers almost more than all the rest put together.

Consumer Report

In rejecting the traditional plaything Mother for a British Standard Rating, the assessors said that it failed only by a narrow margin. Its stuffing was not knocked out of it after 500 test buffetings; the eyes of the newer toughened model did not come out on stalks no matter what treatment it received, and its running costs were on the whole low, though some models needed an increasing amount of lubrication as they grew older. It was felt, however, that the finish wore badly, lacked polish and tended to become too abrasive after prolonged nursery use.

Report from special correspondent Gavin Lyall:

The report of the Kuchold Committee on Wife-Swapping, published today, has produced shocked reactions on its major recommendation: that Brighton should become London's third wife-swapping centre. Existing facilities in NW1 and Chelsea would be exhausted by 1980, the report claims. The first runaway in Brighton should be available two years before that date.

Mr Justice Kuchold, committee chairman, defended the report against accusations of bias. 'We tried it everywhere,' he said in an exclusive interview from a rest-home last night. 'At Cublington, Foulness and in the back of a coach going home from the Cup Final. But we agreed unanimously that Brighton was best.'

Explaining why the committee took so long to report, he said they had been fair to a fault. The fifteen members, each married, had spent precisely one month with each other's partners. 'You can work out for yourself how long that would take,' Justice Kuchold said. 'And so could I, once.'

Mrs Jenny Talls, another committee member, said that all the meetings had been 'almost without friction'. The only problem had arisen when one member swapped another's wife for a bottle of Japanese whisky in Limehouse. Tokyo police had been alerted to look for her, 'and we accept,' said Mrs Talls, 'that the member concerned may honestly have misunderstood the committee's terms of reference.'

Filth

Oh gawd, now the sun's out – so I can't see through the windows. Why this should be so is science, and therefore, like the windows, impenetrable; but the one thing about which I don't want my consciousness raised right now is filth. What the eye doesn't see the heart doesn't have to make unreliable plans to do something about.

Depends whose eye, of course. When I clear the kitchen there are half a dozen surfaces that have to be wiped off, after which I reckon the place is perfect – or it would be if it wasn't for the junk the others have left: a boomerang, modelling glue, a typewriter huddling against the radiator for warmth. But *they* don't see it as junk. The typewriter is Work, so that's OK, the boomerang isn't *lost*, I knew it was there; and anyway what about those saucers left on the floor full of fossils and what looks like yoghurt? Oh, those. They are the cat saucers. They don't count, or at any rate I don't see them. Much discord, I suspect, could be avoided if couples knew which the areas of marital blindness were: might try leaving a card saying I HAVE A LOVER in a different place each day, and noting when the blow-up came.

I suppose if one didn't have selective eyes one would go bananas, but the amount of dirt you're conditioned to accept does vary. Babies, who almost never cart coal or play football are bathed each morning and even get their hair washed, at least until they get a scaly scalp and someone says don't be an idiot. One dabs obsessively at one's children with a wet cloth until about the time they go to school, but it's not that they then learn to keep themselves clean, it's just that they give one something more interesting to worry about.

Whether women wash is a very touchy subject, not much enriched by statistical truth: I once heard of a man who said '50 per cent of the women I've slept with wash afterwards' and when his wife said what the hell, he said: 'Well you do, and the other one didn't.' I remember discovering a whole new place in my ears when I was about 15, and as I don't suppose the ears develop much at puberty, I imagine they'd lain unwashed since my mother had stopped scrubbing me. And if I don't bath as often as I'd like, I certainly wash a whole lot more thoroughly now, as I step gloomily off the scales trying to persuade myself my bedsocks weigh 4 lb. each, than I ever did in the days when I bathed every morning. All *that* meant was sitting in hot water for fifteen minutes without even wetting my neck.

The dirt on men is even more peculiar. One man I'm related to has no rim round his shirt collar after five days, another changes his shirt every hour on the hour, is rarely seen washing but *never* niffs. A schoolboy will polish his shoes and go off proudly, oblivious of the shoe polish still on his wrists; and many a man fusses frantically about the spotless collar over which he hangs his greasy hair.

But it doesn't do to get obsessed with these things. One of the best things the magazine *Over 21* ever did was to set a psychiatrist on to that ghastly woman in the TV ads who goes on and on about the germs round the S-bend. The medics may have started all the stuff about germs, but now that we know that lice live so close to the scalp they don't care about the length of the hair waving above them, and that hundreds of life-forms infest even the best of us, it's surely time we stopped fussing about inner cleanliness.

Since anyway you will never know whether you caught your germ from the dust in the cupboard or because the cat sat on the draining-board, the great thing seems to be to avoid anyone realising how grubby you really are. And here comes

Thomas Hardy, keen observer of the Dorset poor, with the answer. It is, he says, a question of *colour*. 'I always kip a white apron behind the door to slip on when the gentlefolk knock, for if so be they see a white apron they think ye be clane,' said a woman with a floor like a pigeon loft; while those homes favouring brown and amber tones were 'thought necessarily the abode of filth and Giant Despair'. Hardy didn't think being clean meant being happy anyway, I may say – like the cheerful soul who said that in his case cleanliness wasn't so much next to godliness as next to impossible.

Possibly it's our consciousness of pollution on a giant scale that somehow puts the fluff under the bed in perspective; possibly it's the realisation that total purity is a pretty unobtainable goal – like those United States housewives in Betty Friedan's book, who, on acquiring an automatic washing machine, simply washed the sheets twice a week instead of once. When I get my ideal of the ten-day week, we will all change the sheets thirty-six times a year instead of fifty-two, and nobody will ever know the difference. In any case, surely an age in which I say: 'I'm writing about filth this week' and they all think I'm getting my knife into Mary Whitehouse again must be altogether too clean by half?

Best Friend Once Removed

With Bob and Carol and Ted and Alice (since I obviously can't give their real names) I enjoy a very curious relationship. Or have a very curious relationship. They are not quite my friends, but I know them better than many who are; they aren't related to me, but they might as well be. They are the close friends of *my* close friends – my friends-in-law.

I know too much about them, and try very hard to forget they must know too much about me. Sometimes, of course, the mutual friends wrap it up a bit, give one the full histoire without mentioning the names: 'What she can't stand is he just won't mention money, she doesn't mind the gambling but he simply won't discuss it'; or 'he realises she does like living it up but I doubt if he really knows. . . .' Then all you have to do is to discover, with a carefully casual question, *who* it was they spent the weekend before last with and you know it all. Then when you next meet these friends of friends you feel as edgy as if you'd been reading their diaries.

And they have far too much power to throw one off balance. On a bad day, what cheers you along is not, let's face it, the fact that your mother loves you – she just might not be entirely without bias. It is the fact that, whatever I am like – bad at soufflés and good at scrambled eggs, Eurobust 40, fond of potatoes, given to forgetting people's names after the third drink and puffing into the office thirty seconds before deadline – with all my faults, there are a chosen few who think I'm great. And they are persons of judgement; well, obviously, they must be.

But they admire those awful others too, that's what undermines the whole thing. For if the friends-in-law are witty and gay and attractive, it makes you wonder if, actually, you are the B-team of your trusted chums. If they're coarse and self-deceiving, nasty, brutish and short, you suddenly wonder if the judgment of the dear chums can be that good after all.

Should the friends-in-law be yawningly heavy in the mind and drone endlessly about Kafka, you feel even more illiterate than usual; if however, they are utter light-weights with nothing between or behind the ears but Diorissimo, you can't help the dreadful feeling that it's you who are the heavy, just waiting for the conversation to come round to some sombre topic like Rhodesia or education.

Of course it's illogical; one knows perfectly well that friends need only meet one facet of oneself completely. He's the only man in England who can talk about guns for three hours without drawing a breath; she's the only woman in the road who shouts at her children louder than I do; it forms a bond. It's hardly to be expected that the gun-nutter has *no* other interests – in cost-accounting, say, or cricket; yet you still can't bear to share the evening with this other friend of his – the great beery business man in the I. Zingari sweater. And I never bothered what she did before she was married – until suddenly there's this piece of fluff from her old modelling school and they're shrieking and giggling about their darkroom past.

You might think the answer was simply to move in and adopt the people as proper friends of your own; but even this has pitfalls. If you're making a friend cold, from the outside world, you can quarrel or go off them without repercussions; but if you do it to a friend of a friend, it's as bad as jilting your cousin.

When it does work, of course, it's delightful; since, whichever one you're with, you can spend time cosily picking over the other: friends should ideally be in threes, like revolutionary cells, for this reason. Indeed there are one or two people who seem put into this world solely for the purpose of giving all their friends a chance to ring up one another and discuss what should best be done about poor X; one suspects that if poor X ever *did* pull himself together, as advised, get off pot and onto a payroll, and stop trailing his bedraggled sex life all over London, we would all secretly resent the removal of so good a topic of conversation.

The only consolation is that in the end, whatever they're like the process takes place with friends-in-law as it does with neighbours and real relations, with workmates and flatmates and very old cats: if you have disliked them long enough, you really become quite fond of them.

You may still wish you had the original friends to yourself, but if you were honest you'd admit, as the man said about the froth on the beer (at least my family believe it was about froth on beer), 'Funny, you know Bill, it's all that stands between you and yer 'appiness, yet you'd grumble if it wasn't there.'

Misprint Eyes

It all started with MOVE TO BEAUTIFY CARDINAL. Lovely, I thought, deep eye shadow, roses round the red cap. Then I saw they'd actually written 'beatify'; all they wanted was to make him into a boring old saint. The next time it was a poster for a musician called Earl Fatha Hines; but I'd already invented a long scenario to go with Earl's Father Hides – and wondered, indeed, how an Earl could have a living father; maybe he had wrongly assumed the title just because Dad was lurking in a chalk pit. But it had been such a curious name, anyway, I thought nothing of it.

Lately, though, it's been getting worse. I don't count all the times I've read advertisements for shoplifters, because the word's almost the same as shopfitters. I'm prepared to admit there may be Freudian implications in thinking the David Hockney film was called, not *A Bigger Splash* but *A Bugger's Plash*, or that 'The Feeling to Start Soon in Hampstead' was what the headline said not Tree Felling. But when it came to Secret Plans to Reorganise Ducks (like swan-upping only *worse*) instead of docks, I began to suspect it was time I did something about my eyes.

This little complaint is not quite the same as the sort of Paul Jennings misconstructions that afflict one in the normal way – things like supposing the thriller *The List of Adrian Messenger* to be about a chap who leaned dangerously to one side; or that the last five words of the ad 'If you were asked which was the world's greatest newspaper you would probably say *The Times*. Have you read it recently?' were meant to be spoken on a note of rising incredulity. And it's a bit different from noting all those charming west country villages with names like Chipping Norton,

Chipping Sodbury, Loose Chippings; or Compton Dando, Upper Cowleaze, Parking Toilets. Nor does simply mis-reading the words put one in the way of constructing new ones like Barbara Griggs's Insinuendo, or my new one Freudulent.

But all the same I mostly prefer what I read to what they're written. I'm not the sex to get much of a charge out of Topless Jobs One Million, but it's a pleasant thought; Making a Movie to Sack Alan Sapper from ACTT – well, it might make a splendid feature film. It seemed entirely accurate to see the 'designated' police super for an airport apparently described as Chief Superintendent Divisional Commander (desperate) of Airport Police; and Secondhand Cats Bought and Sold suggests this marvellous compound full of waving tails and whiskers, the shoppers treading delicately among them – much better than a few hard-faced car dealers.

When it came to the point where I could hardly read a book in bed without my eyes swimming, though, I finally went to the occulist; and he made me read these bits of Polish they put up on the wall, and sat me down kindly and explained that, as one grows older, the point of focus does move farther away from the eyes. 'I see,' I said with quiet resignation. 'So you think I should have glasses?' 'No,' he said. 'I think you should hold the book farther from your face.'

So there the matter rests; except that something even more alarming has begun to happen. My typewriter's starting spelling 'editor' as 'idiotr' which will only get me into trouble; and now I think it's spreading to my *ears*. The other day I walked into a room to hear someone saying, 'But it takes so long to get an actor mended . . .' and I had visions of all those broken puppets in the hospital before I realised he meant 'to get an Act amended. . . .' Where is it all going to end?